A JOURNEY TO THE UNITED STATES OF AMERICA

EDITED VERSION

BY

CHRISTOPH KOMLA ANKUVIE

Brilliant Books Literary
137 Forest Park Lane Thomasville
North Carolina 27360 USA

ACKNOWLWEDGMENTS

To begin with, I would like to thank Almighty God who saw all my father's children through the hard moments when we were growing in those days at Akposso Bibi in Togo.

Secondly, this book would not have seen the light without meeting Mr. Wisdom Sagoe and Mrs. Patience Sagoe popularly known as Sister Pat. It is good to know people in life because you might never know when to fall on them for help.

They took care of me at Wa in Upper West Region of Ghana over a period of six months until I received my first salary as a French Teacher in 1998.

Furthermore, from the bottom of my heart, I want to thank Miss Vincentia Votere and her entire family members for their numerous hospitality services during my three years stay at Wa in Upper West Region of Ghana.

It is worth to note that Mr. Wisdom Sagoe and Vincentia Votere are the source of the opportunity that brought me to the United States of America.

At this juncture, I would like to mention Mr. Komla Penty and his wife Stephanie Arnold Penty. With the help of Mr. Komla, the wife agreed to provide me with Affidavit of support, which enables me to get Visa from American Embassy in Ghana.

I am equally grateful to Elikplim who has hosted me in Uptown Chicago, after Mr. Komla Penty took care of me for a period of time. He is the one who shared the idea of joining the United States Navy with me.

Last but not the least, I am sincerely grateful to my immediate supervisor—Mr. Al Martin (CS1), for taking his time to read through this manuscript. Mr. Al was the leading Petty Officer in NAS Admiral Nimitz Galley (Oak Harbor) at the time I was writing this book. He deserves my gratitude for an outstanding job well done.

Finally, I wish to express my sincere thanks to my brother Dr. Ankuvie Augustine. He is the devoted brother who has decided to finance the opportunity that came my way while I was teaching French Language at Fallahia JSS at Wa in Upper West Region in Ghana.

Without Dr. Ankuvie's commitment to finance the chance I got I would not have been in position to make the journey to U.S A. May God continues to bless him in all his endeavors.

DEDICATION

This book is dedicated to my parents, guardians, brothers, and sisters. My father, Edward Mensah Ankuvie, deserves every credit. He instilled the sense of self discipline in us right from an early stage that reflected in us. He believes in "Spare the rod, spoil the child." He passed away in 1998, may his soul rest in eternal peace.

My mother is called Florence Atieku. She is privately known as "Da Kosua." She comes from Anfoega-Dzana in the Volta Region of Ghana.

The name of my second mother who has been the pivot of our success is Gladys Mama Tokoe Ankuvie. She is from my father's village, Wusuta. Had it not been for her constant and persistent motivation, as well as strong words of encouragement for all of us, none of us would be where we are today. She is popularly referred to as "Nana."

They taught us how to endure both the good and the bad moments that might come our way. My brothers, sisters, and I all understood the need to have come from parents and guardians who were uneducated yet wanted to equip us with the best tool to deal with life in unprecedented occurrences.

In so doing, we listened to their day-to-day pieces of advice. I am grateful to them and looking back at where we started from, I am convinced beyond reasonable doubt that their efforts have not been wasted in any way. More grease to their elbow.

CONTENTS

PREFACE

This book is about me—Christoph Komla Ankuvie-an African child's struggle of the past, and how I got here in the United States of America on the fifth of July, 2000. It is equally depicting what my brothers, sisters, and I have all gone through in order to arrive at our present stage. I believe that there are uncounted fellow human beings who are in the world (community, society) experiencing the same or similar circumstances. Your present life situations may be threatened by your next meal, shelter to lay your head, clothing to wear, money to finance your education, etc. All hopes may turn into endless frustrations and what have you not. In the middle of all these, do not give up, but continue to endure.

As I am writing this book, I am proud to inform you that I have a Bachelor of Science Degree in Business Administration from Colorado Technical University with the concentration in Business Management. I left the shore of Ghana on the fourth of July, America's Republic Day, and got to the United States of America on the fifth of July, 2000. My host at Chicago convinced me to practice Buddhism with him as a shortcut to get a job. Within a few days, one female member of the chanting group assisted me in getting a job for me at the Ritz-Carton Chicago, a Four Seasons Hotel downtown, as an overnight housekeeper. On the seventeenth of July, 2000, I was hired and I began working in the hotel. I made a crucial decision to join the United States Navy on the twenty-fifth of October 2000.

By the time you finish reading this book, you will learn a lot about how African children toil so as to grow. In African continent there are fifty-four countries. Each of them is an individual nation. By then, there was no state of union, unlike the United States of America. I want you the reader to see how far I have come from the use of machete in the village in Togo and Ghana, my country of origin to the pursuit of the American Dream. My brothers, sisters, and I all began life in Togo in a thick forest with no electricity or potable water, not to mention the use of a telephone in time of emergency, but by the grace of Almighty God, I am now living in the United States of America pursuing my American dream.

Furthermore, I would like to let you know that life is full of surprises, miracles, and what have you not. Some people are therefore born with a silver spoon in their mouths while others have to work hard for it. That was my case including my brothers and sisters, under the care of our mother, popularly called Mama Tokoe. I don't know about yours. It is not all the time that things have to work for you smoothly the way you wish them to be. You may be facing some challenges, hard times, frustrations, loneliness, depression, etc. In the middle of these, please don't give up, but rather gather hope and continue to endure the pain. I promise you of a better future.

Looking back in retrospect, having reflected upon my life, I feel there is a need to bring the experiences of my siblings and me into writing. This has led me to come out with this book titled "A Journey to the United States of America."

Sometimes your community thinks you have enough to give extra, yet in actual, you are out of means. Imagine when you are doing well and all of sudden you lose your source of income, at the same time you have to cater for your family. Your immediate society continues to hail you, thinking you still have funds while, in actual fact, there is a war going within yourself. Such was the story of my father. That is the time innocent children are born. Their needs have to be attended to. It is an incredible story and a remarkable one indeed. Never give up, keep on trying. That is to say, no matter how dark the night is, there will be a brighter day ahead.

Your story may seem to be out of the frying pan and into fire. Wait until you hear the story of other people. Others are from simple to complex or vice versa. Whatever your case may be, I am sure God is in control. Can you imagine being born into a family of twelve, and you are the eighth child from the bottom. You now have a picture of what was in my mind, including pain, agony and the dedication to strive for a better future.

But something happened that dramatically changed my life and that of my brothers and sisters. I am sure you would like to know what transpired in my life either positively or negatively. In the course of reading this book, you will come across what really occurred to me. Have you ever heard the saying "Humble yourself and the Lord will lift you high? We all went through the hard moments and self-discipline and endurance was a key factor.

As you read this book, it is my sincere desire that you will come across something that would one day move you to push yourself forward. Don't think you are the only one out there that is suffering. As you suffer today, I am optimistic that you are building your future. You are not actually suffering, but rather sowing a seed which later will germinate and grow for you to harvest. In other words, you are laying a solid foundation for your future. Listen to your parents and guardians. They are your first teachers. Of course, seek formal education. Enjoy this book.

INTRODUCTION

There comes a time in the life of mankind where you need, or you have to take stock of your own life like how a prosperous businessman does. Some people call it inventory taking or pondering over your life. I feel every human being should reflect or go into himself or herself and see how he or she is doing at a point in time.

Such a moment came into my life when, all of sudden, opportunity knocked at my door in Ghana, my country of origin, and I grabbed it firmly for a greener pasture in the United States of America. Sitting down on the couch at home in America after work reminds me of where I began from. It also tells me of how you may not actually plan for an event, but it can come your way positively or negatively.

When it happens like that, some people begin to ask a series of questions such as who is that person! Is he or she not that farmer's son or daughter? How did he or she get the opportunity for a change? You can think of the list of questions. In the middle of it all, I want to let such people know that yes, you may be that boy or girl growing in the village or living in the next door, but Almighty God has plans for all of us at the appropriate time.

The young ones shall grow to be adults one day. I don't know about you, but in my case, I would say my brothers as well as sisters all have come a long way and looking back at where we started from, I feel I should put our experiences into writing. When you are born from parents who are rich and you don't have to suffer or go through any form of struggle in order to grow, in a sense, it is good, and everyone may wish to have come from such a home. But that would not be the case for every child in life. What if your parents are middle income workers with a lot of kids to take care of? Sometimes, you could be born from a father who was once rich but is out of resources when majority of his children are born.

Such was the case of my father a one-time cocoa farmer and purchaser who was rich with three kids and when nine other siblings were born, he became financially weak. However, that was a moment for more responsibilities. Can you dodge the reality of the time? Honestly speaking, I don't think so. Life must go on. The children must be catered for in one way or the other. They have to go to school, eat, be clothed, etc.

Being a child born into that type of a large family, you have to open your eyes and think of certain things that no one knows about. You can now see where my brothers, sisters, and I are all coming from. It requires dedication not only from parents and guardians but from the young ones too. There were personal issues bothering me. It is what I will describe as the war within myself. How could our parents meet the demands of nine of us? Outsiders thought my father was still rich, yet it is only we the kids in the house who knew what was actually going on. Can you imagine parents with no formal educational background, yet are willing to educate their children?

Going to school requires us to assist our father on the farm in order to get what we needed. We quickly realized the need to listen and do exactly as he instructed us to do. By so doing, we all got the various support of our parents and guardians. It tells me that your present situations could be changed based on your own approach and personal understanding. You can either better or worsens your plights depending upon your own initiative. Nothing comes easy in this life until you decide to make it easy for yourself.

In case you are born today, and you find life so easy and everything seems to be working for you smoothly, don't forget that the people who have gone before you are the ones who have paved the way for you. You cannot build a house without first setting up a solid foundation.

It goes on to say that nothing comes in an easy way. You have to work for it assiduously. There is also no cheap way to make life more affordable if only you are ready to endure the hardships of it. But when you toil persistently with all your efforts, no wonder the end result will pay off definitely. To me, when circumstances prompt you to suffer at an early stage, it shall serve to you as a yardstick to be more cautious in your subsequent events. People who have therefore accomplished a lot in life all have a story to tell. Majority of them began on a rough note, and with sheer determination, they made it in one way or the other. Having everything on a silver platter without knowing how to work for it is not a recommended path to go down. Mankind should learn how to suffer before enjoying at a tender age and face its consequences later.

There are stories of families who are so rich to the extent that their children don't have to do anything in the form of suffering. Such families even have maid servants for their kids. But the question is when the unexpected happens, can the young ones survive on their own? People who want to make it in life the cheap way must be prepared to pay for consequences. When you suffer before getting a clear chance, it is then that you would know how to hold onto it firmly.

Achieving your God given talents and destiny in life would require you to be in position to first identify where you are coming from, how you got to your present and the future you want for yourself. Many times, when God helps people to advance forward, some of them quickly forget of the past and start making silly mistakes as if they are done in life. You must humble yourself as well so that Almighty God can lift you high. To humble yourself, you need undeniable self-discipline.

When you are self-disciplined, the understanding is that you are ready to do everything to the desirable limit. Self-discipline will remind you to spend money to the limit and have fun to the full but be within the confinement of the law. Sitting down without doing anything meaningful is not a good measure of self-discipline. However, whatever you intend to do, make sure it is within your capabilities. It is a fact that you may be frustrated or there could be a loss of hope when things are not working for you the way you wish it to be. All that I want to say to you, dear reader, is to hang in there. There is a better tomorrow awaiting you someday.

In the course of pursuing your dreams, beware that you will encounter many obstacles that might make you feel that you are forgotten, unwanted, neglected, etc. All doors could be shut at you. Does that mean you should surrender? The answer is an emphatic no! But keep on making the necessary effort so as to alleviate your own agony. If things were so easy for everyone, why is it that everybody has not found what he or she is looking for in the world? That alone should tell you that the world in which we are in is based on certain basic rules and fundamental human principles.

The choices you decide to make in life matter in the long run. If you choose to obey simple and basic rules of life, it would be better for you than the other side of the coin. Gone are those days when you can be the only person that will be judged as the best in a large group. These days, it is rather the opposite. Of late, it is more than just a mere competition. There are many people who are fully prepared to face life in many ways. They are well qualified and when you find yourself in that type of group, you may have to take a step further to strive harder in order to be chosen among the best.

Furthermore, I want you to realize that situations can prompt you to leave what you love or hold so dearly and travel or move to a far place in order to better your future. When such a thing happens to you, do not be worried, rather accept it in good faith. You may have to leave your beloved one, girlfriend, boyfriend, brothers, sisters, parents, guardians, and friends, in general, behind in order to pursue your ambitions elsewhere.

Do not hesitate to make an optimistic decision in your life. What you need to know is that an opportunity comes but once in life while friends and relatives will be there forever. I wanted to stay close to my father's home after I completed teacher training college so as to teach, but because" man proposes, and God disposes" I rather ended up in the far northern part of my country. I did not like it that my wishes were not granted at that time. I was crying when I was going to teach in the northern part of Ghana, little did I know that God has something in store for me over there!

Knowing people and making friends is an awesome thing to do because you may not know when to fall on them for help. I found out that the more you are together today will be the happier you are likely to meet in nature. You would never know when exactly you may meet known friends. It could be one month, six months, a year, or several years. The most important thing is to be on good terms because the future is uncertain. It has a lot of surprises and shocks.

I recently met a secondary school friend of mine whom I had not seen since we completed school in 1993. We happened to complete school in 1993. The two of us attended Kpando Secondary School in the Volta Region of Ghana. While I was in house five in the boys' dormitory, he was in house two. After that, everyone went his or her own way. Imagine meeting him face to face in 2008? He is in the Ghanaian Navy based in Sekondi-Takoradi. I was overwhelmed to see him!

At the time while I was going to secondary school, my mind was not matured enough to have plans as to what I was going to do after school. Neither did I have a goal or a vision for my future. I was just an average student, not gifted child as compared to some of my colleagues. Few things that happened to me after secondary school and I ended up in training college, made me to realize that some people have straightforward routes while others have serpentine roads all leading to their various destinations.

I noticed that I fell into the category of people who have a serpentine path to making life. I realized how I wanted a place to be stationed but did not get it. Among all the people who promised to help me in one way or the other disappointed me. Only a few kept their promises. I ended up where I did not want as a last resort. Today, looking back, I am beginning to understand the plans of God for mankind.

It is true that you would never know what God has in store for you at any point in time. Based on my own experiences, I want to say that failures that might come your way are blessings to you later in your life. You may not be in position to detect it right away. Only time can tell. Whenever you are passing through rough moments, it could be that your God is preparing you for greater things ahead of you. It also means that God does not want you to go down to a certain path. I wanted to remain in the southern part of my country to teach, but God's plans for me took me to the northern part of Ghana and there I met an opportunity to travel to the United States of America.

As you can see, a particular failure at a point in time, was rather to redirect you to your given path. Accept that bad moment of yours in good faith and wait for the Lord to show you where exactly to pass in order to reconnect you to your dreams, goals, and plans. Waiting for God's guidance does not mean you should sit down unconcern either. Keep on trying your gifts of nature on something meaningful until the right time comes. I believe that everyone is created with a special gift, and it will not come out of you easily until you learn how to put your load on your knee for God to assist you carry it on your head. Talking about failures, it happened to me personally when I completed secondary school. A difference of one mark made it impossible for me to advance to the next level of my studies. I was compelled to retake exams for a year and made the grade in the required subject before moving on with my academic life. When I was ready to move on, I lost interest in my previous choice and decided to try my luck on teacher training college which was not my original plans.

As you can see it in my own case, your situations may seem to be similar or worse than others. In the middle of it all, you must exercise a great deal of patience. It is not going to be easy but try as much as possible to contain it and the pain or anger that comes with it. I personally felt that my friends bypassed me at a point in time. I also felt rejected. Life was meaningless to me. I was equally frustrated and isolated. I was ashamed of myself and desperate, but there was nothing I could do about it. Such is nature and I have to deal with that emotional trouble for a year.

Wait until you hear the stories of other people, and you would be amazed a lot. Your rough and bad moments in your life can eventually shape you to become a better person the young ones would like to grow to be one day. Others shall see you as a source of worthy inspiration.

All of sudden, you will become a role model in society. You can now occupy a top position in your community. The world will start hailing you at a higher price. The world is your immediate society in which you reside. That is to say that some people will begin consulting your point of view on important issues bordering them. How you struggled before getting to that stage, it is only you and your personal God who is aware of it.

Taking my bag and traveling to the United States of America sounds rosy to anyone who has not been to America before. How to board the airplane from Kotoka International Airport in Ghana might be the easiest thing. Wait until you arrive in America. How to settle, get a job and adjust to the American environment is another thing to deal with. Your accent as an immigrant who speaks multiple languages from your native land is equally a big factor.

The mentality of a cross section of people living in a developing country is that anyone coming to America is going to be rich. They have forgotten about all the difficulties you have to go through in order to get a job. As soon as you inform them that you are eventually working, the phone would start ringing. The next thing is to send them money. I am beginning to understand some of the reasons why some rich people would not like to let their money go. If only you know the way and manners in which they toiled before getting their resources, you would not like to criticize them. Since one good turn deserves another, I will appeal to you to help mankind despite all that you might have gone through in order to arrive at your present place. It is God who has seen you through all your struggles, not by your own power anyway. Also, don't forget too that the same place you pass to climb a tree, mostly, it should be that same place you have to pass to come down.

That is to say that, at any given moment in life, there is always someone whom God is going to use to assist you in one way or the other. The very people who assisted you while climbing the tree of life must be remembered. You never know what the future holds in store for you. As such, be prepared at all times. Don't ever forget about where you came from, why you have to move or travel and how you got here. If you do, posterity shall question your conscience forever. Finally, use your personal judgment wisely in whatever blessing that may come your way to help mankind in a small way in glorifying Almighty God in heaven.

MY CHILDHOOD LIFE

My name is Christoph Komla Ankuvie. I come from Ghana in West Africa. I am now living in the United States of America. I was born on the seventeenth of November 1970, in a place called Dodi-Papase, a village in the Jasikan District in the Volta Region of Ghana. My father's name is Edward Mensah Ankuvie (died in 1998), a cocoa farmer in Akposso Bibi in the Republic of Togo. My mother's name is Florence Akosua Atieku from Anfoega Dzana in the Volta Region of Ghana. My other mother's name is (Stepmother) Gladys Ankuvie, popularly known as Mama Tokoe or Nana for short. She is the woman who stood by our father to make it happen for us. Even though we are from Ghana, we were all living in Togo at that time.

My mother gave birth to my sister Edith Ankuvie and myself then she moved on with her life without my father. That was the story I grew up to be told. I do not know the details of that story to tell you. My father gave birth to twelve of us and nine of the twelve including myself were living with my stepmother at that moment. The first three children were also living with their mother at the Ghana-Togo border town known as Kute. In total, my father had twelve of us from four different women three from one woman, one from another

15

woman, two of us from my mother, and the other six from Mama Tokoe (my stepmother).

I happened to be the eighth child among my father's twelve children from the bottom. The nine of us who were under the care of Mama Tokoe attended a Roman Catholic primary School in Akposso Bibi in Togo. The school's name is Ecole Primaire Catholique de Bibi. I could not recollect the exact year I went to primary school in Togo. However, I can remember my first day at school. Those days, when you are due to start attending school, you will be accompanied by either your mother or father to school. As you arrived at the school, you would be directed to the office of the head teacher.

The next thing I remembered was that the head teacher held my hand over my head in order to reach my left ear. At that time, when your hand was not able to reach your left ear, you will be asked to go home until the following year. Fortunately for me, I passed that particular test and was admitted into school. I went through six years of primary education. We had to walk maybe four to five miles in order to go to school every day. My two brothers by the names Augustine and Moses, Mawuse, Paul, myself, Hellen, Edith, and Faustine all attended the same school before going to continue in Ghana.

Early at down, my mother would ensure that we are awake so that we could be at school on time. When we woke up, we had to wash our face, rinse our mouth and chew "atidudu" It is a local stick that served the purpose of brushing out teeth. We had morning and afternoon school sessions. After the morning session, we walked back home to eat. Within one hour after eating, we had to do house assignments such as going to the cocoa farm to fetch firewood and going to the thick forests to weed plantation farms, as well as walking a few miles to the riverside to fetch drinking water with buckets and pots. By 2:00 P.M, we had to get ready to go back to school.

Life in Akposso Bibi by then was a typical village one. Every farmer established his house in the middle of his or her cocoa farm. We were living in the middle of a thick forest. In the night, all that you could see was darkness. There was nothing like electricity to think about. There was no source of potable water. We had to drink water from the river that was flowing with all the germs in it. The only time we drank good water was when the rain fell heavily, and we happened to collect it into the various barrels my parents had with big pots.

At night we used kerosene lamps or torch lights in order to see and cook. The day we ran out of kerosene, the only lamp that had a little bit of kerosene would be utilized to enable my mother to do the cooking and that meant we had to sleep in darkness. As you may notice, it rains mostly in the forest areas. The day it rains so heavy, the river we crossed on our way to school would be overflowing the big log that was cut and placed across it. When such a thing happened, on that day or a couple of days, we could not go to school. If you tried to cross the river, you could be gone. It is as simple as that.

We did our night studies with kerosene lamps. My father's major source of income was from his cocoa farm works. He made good money from his cocoa products. Out of that, he was able to build two houses: one at the Ghana-Togo border town by the name Kute, and a big house at home in Wusuta in Ghana. He was respected in the area. He was at one time, a purchasing agent for a number of cocoa marketing companies. One of them was based in a popular city of Togo by the name of Atakpame.

At the time my father had money, the nine of us that I spoke earlier on about that were under my stepmother's care had not been born yet. The first three born from another woman, apart from my stepmother, were enjoying the good moment of our father. When the nine of us came into the picture, his cocoa buying business collapsed due to what I believe was financial mismanagement. We had to face the reality of the time. A lot of responsibilities fell on Mama Tokoe.

She had to sell hair products in that time known as "Yombo." Early in the morning she would go to the market to make money and buy necessary things needed for the house. She went to a different market each day of the week. On Monday, she went to a market in Dzogbegan. Tuesdays are Kute market days. She attended the market at Manguasi on Wednesday. Thursday, she went to the market at Badou, and on Fridays, she was at Bena's market. Most of the time, she came back late. She has to walk in order to cross a river before attending Kute's market.

Basically, she applied the end products to the hair of her customers and the color changes to black. Every Friday was the market day for the area. Around eight a.m people would start emerging from everywhere, and by noon the market was in full session. When we broke from school at noon, we all went to the market. Sometimes we were late for the afternoon session.

Anytime you are late to school, you would receive a minimum of four whippings on your buttocks. Some other times, the head teacher would ask you to kneel down for a possible half of an hour. Other punishments for lateness to school included weeding school plots with a cutlass, bringing a load of firewood to school, sweeping classrooms, cleaning, and doing any type of dirty work for your teacher in his or her house. The teachers of that time had a lot of authority, and if you dared to refuse to take their orders, you could imagine what would happen to you.

I remembered that we had to use a cutlass to weed the soccer field that we had. There was nothing like a mower to cut for us. Some of the teachers, including the head teacher, used us to work on their private farms for monetary gains. We fetched them firewood from our father's cocoa farm. We used ropes to tie the firewood and carried it on our heads while walking to school, with one hand supporting the load and the other hand holding our school bag. If you don't have a school bag, then you had to hold your books in your hand. You can imagine the anxieties of such an African child who is now in United States of America. What a story! You need to read on. You have not yet come to what is probably the most exiting aspect of my story. Let me go back to my story.

In the middle of the village life, my brothers, sisters, and I were going through we were happy kids running around playing in the rain and moonlight and swimming in the flowing river. There was no thought of asking for a better life with electricity, potable water, etc

Whenever celebrations like Christmas, New Year, and Easter were coming, we were already in the mood of enjoyment. Our mother Mama-Tokoe always made it possible for us to feel loved. She really played an incredible role in the life of the nine of us that were under her care. I could recollect that by September to the ending of October, she had already gotten ready for Christmas festivities that were coming.

I bet you that she would buy materials and send us to tailor shop for measurement. When the outfits were ready, we were there to try them on and retrieved them for the upcoming merrymaking. My brother Paul and I would sneak into the room when our mother was not around to admire our Christmas dress. We had to hide whenever we did that because when we were caught tampering with them, we would have been in trouble even though the dresses belonged to us. We were only allowed to have them on fresh on that faithful merrymaking day. Usually, we had two outfits, one for Christmas and the other for the New Year celebration.

Paul and I normally had outfits with the same colors while my other two brothers by the name Koku Moses and Komla Augustine, who is now Dr. Ankuvie of Donkorkroam Hospital in Afram Plains in Ghana, wore new dresses made with the same colors. My sisters also, wore outfits of the same kind that were called in those days by the name "An-Ko." It is a local terminology which means two or more people wearing an outfit that has the same resemblance.

The name of my sisters are as follows; Ankuvie Mawuse Pauline, Ankuvie Babe Hellen, Ankuvie Yawavi Edith (she died in 1999 and left behind a boy, Kossi, and a girl by the name Jennifer), Ankuvie Enyonam Faustine, and Ankuvie Nana Philomina. My father's first three children I spoke of earlier on that lived at Kute in a Ghanaian border town with their mother are: Ankuvie Matilda, Ankuvie Kofi Patrick (he died in Barcelona, Spain in 1990 in search of greener pasture). The third one is called Ankuvie Comfort.

On Christmas Eve, our mother would ask us to slaughter a few goats and lambs bought from Akposso Bena market for preparations toward the merrymaking day. Mama Tokoe also ordered us to catch and slaughter some fowls and cocks which we used to raise in the village. Nana had a small poultry coop. It was a kind of an outside free-range system. It is a system whereby poultry birds and animals are able to roam freely outdoors rather than being confined by an enclosure for some hours a day.

On Christmas day, which is the twenty fifth of December, is often celebrated with a lot of merry making from attending church services to a midnight disco dance and traditional dance known as borborbor. Early in the morning, we were already in a jubilation mood. Some people did not even go to bed the night before. Our mother Mama Tokoe would instruct everyone and together we all helped in the cooking process. The first dish we cooked in the morning was "Fufu." It is a local food that is made from cassava tubes uprooted from the soil. You peel off the skin of the cassava and cut it open into halves, wash thoroughly and then place in a pot over a source of heat and add cold water to it. You let it boil maybe thirty-five to forty minutes until it is cooked. The next thing you do is to pound it in a mortar with a pestle until the end result becomes smooth with a brown color in case you add plantain to it. At that stage that I just described, the fufu is ready for consumption. It is usually formed into balls. Fufu is a staple food common in West African Countries.

While the cassava is being pounded in a mortar with pestle, the slaughtered goats, sheep, and chicken's meats are used to make light soups. Basically, the various meats are placed in a big copper or pot with little water. You then chopped some fresh onions, tomatoes, peppers, grounded ginger and other spices into it. Add salt, chicken or beef seasoning to it so as to develop a flavor for the soup. At this juncture, cover the pot of soup, and apply heat under it and let it simmer about twenty to twenty-five minutes. As it starts to boil, because it is covered, the steam that is supposed to evaporate into the air is forced to stay in thereby developing an aroma as well as flavor for the soup. In about 20 minutes you may open it and stir the soup, making sure that the bottom meats come to the top and also ensuring that all ingredients are blending in the proper way. After another twenty minutes, you can uncover the soup and add water to it up to the quantity of soup you desire to make.

You should let the soup boil and simmer up to an hour. As it boils, keep on tasting to check the flavor of the soup so that you can add any missing ingredients. By one hour, the end result should constitute a desirable and palatable soup. You can set up a table and fetch the soup into a bowls and the plate of fufu by the side. As a local dish, you have to use your hand to cut it and then dip into the soup. Finally, you swallow it. Fufu is often dipped into the soup and eaten with all kind of meats and vegetables such as okra, and garden egg. As a traditional food, we use hands to eat it and it tastes better that way. It is comparable to having a number of American dishes, just like a hamburger, you have to use your hand to eat it.

As you can see, it is a long process to make fufu. That is why you have to start early in order to finish it on time. After eating fufu, we heat water and poured it into buckets, then carry it to the bathroom for a shower. Whenever we all have taken our baths, we are then allowed to wear our long awaiting new dresses to church service. I remembered my brother Paul and I would walk together with shoulders high and with pride while our brothers, Moses and Augustine too would be in their best dress to church.

Right after church service we come back to the house to start helping our mother to cook dinner. Dinner on Christmas day was rice and stew. When we finished eating the delicious rice and stew made with goat or lamb meat my brother Paul and I were sent to deliver Christmas dishes to our neighbors. By the time we came back to the house, other neighbors too have also brought us food. We the children get so excited and eat until our bellies are full. This act of food sharing is done to show appreciation for friendship and loved ones while we were living in a cottage.

My father will buy us soda, juices, and beer. There was no drinking age issue that I knew of by then so we the kids sometimes hid and consumed alcohol as young as we were. I remembered those days that whenever my father was gone to take a shower, I ran into his bedroom to drink alcohol and quickly came out before getting caught. One day i was telling it to my sister Pauline and she confirmed it to me that she was doing the same thing and we all burst into laughter.

In the evening, we either went to the disco or the traditional dance called borborbor. In some part of Togo, Benin and in the Volta Region of Ghana, the Ewes people are noted for Borborbor and agbadza. It is a local dance organized in the village Chief's house. The villagers all come from near and far. The village chief of the time was called Togbe Well. He was a famous leader and rich as well. Behind his house was the venue. The members of the borborbor group even rehearsed ahead of time very well so as to entertain the large crowd. The folks gathered under the shady tree and beat the various drums while the women sang their part harmoniously to the bit of both the song and the drums.

As they sang the song, some trained women would start dancing in a circular form. The borborbor was always the climax of every celebration in the area. We the young folks loved every bit of it. It was the occasion where we used the opportunity to get connected to ladies that you might have been admiring for a long time. Some of my friends and I waited until it was dark before we joined the crowd to dance. Somewhere along the line, the dancing was interrupted, and local drinks were brought to serve the drummers and the singers. Such drinks were called Akpeteshie and palm wine referred to as "Deha."

The end result of palm wine that is left in a tank for two weeks is distilled and the outcome is called Akpeteshie or Apio for short. It is strong liquor. If you are not careful, you will be intoxicated easily. Around midnight, Togbe Well, the Akposso Bibi village Chief gave orders for the jubilation to come to an end so that the crowd can disperse and go home. That was how we celebrated Christmas in the village. Despite the heavy rainfall, endless sunshine, and darkness, long walks to most place, and fatigue from the cocoa farm works, we had a good time and there was no course for alarm.

Right after the Christmas celebration, we start preparing for New Year. We usually sat by a fire on New Year's Eve. The idea was to say goodbye to the older year and welcome the New Year. More celebration took place just like during the birth of Jesus Christ. The beginning of the New Year in January is when we had to go back to school. We didn't really want to go back to school. But you have to remove the jubilation from your mind and get ready to go back to school.

It is also the era where some parents spent all their money on Christmas celebration thereby forgetting to set aside some money to pay the school fees of their kids. My parents always ensured that they set aside funds to cater for our school needs. Dry season begins in January, marking the end of cocoa season until early August to September and up to December. When we came back from school, we went to the farm to clear forest land from five acres to maybe six so as to sow maize.

This is done manually with cutlasses and axes to cut down big trees. After cutting down the trees and bushes, we allow it to dry for three weeks, and then we set fire to it to burn. You now have the land ready to sow maize. Sometimes, the first rain comes around April. When it rains about five times, then we go to the farm to start sowing maize. At a certain moment, in a two-week period, you need to check whether the seeds sown have germinated.

When your crops germinate and the rainfall pattern has changed, the crops might be damaged by drought. A prolonged drought makes the crops to become badly affected. The mere look at your maize farm can tell you of their wilting point. At this stage, no amount of rainfall can bring the crops back to life. Because of circumstances of that nature, my father always ensured that there was food and financial security by storing grains and other farm commodities ahead of lean season.

The harvest of maize was within three months. We had to provide manual labor to do the hoeing among the stalks as a way of controlling the weeds on the farm. Our farming system was based on subsistence level. That means what we produced could barely support us all year round. By then, there was no scientific way of storing maize harvest to minimize post-harvest loss. In the nutshell, the above constituted some of the activities that my siblings and I were undertaking alongside our primary education while we live in Togo.

MY SECONDARY
SCHOOL DAYS

I am sure I completed six years of primary education around 1984 to 1985 at Akposso-Bibi in Togo. As was the trend, my father brought me to Wusuta which is our hometown in the Volta Region of Ghana in order to continue schooling. By then, Ghana's system of education was the British-based O-Level and A-Level. What it means is that the system consists of six years of primary education followed by four years of middle school before you can go to secondary school.

After four years of middle school, students were asked to write the popular examination of the time by the name Middle School leaving certificate. Candidates who pass it could go to Teacher Training College and other technical schools. While you are in form one, form two, or form three of four years middle school, you can take the common entrance exam as a shortcut, and if you pass it, you were admitted to the secondary school. As I said earlier on, the secondary school was made up of five years of academic studies known as O-Level, and an option of undertaking a two-year six form program referred to as A-Level or Upper Secondary Education.

I attended Wusuta Hotor L/A Middle School. The head teacher by then nicknamed Master Prota conducted an interview for me in his office. He told me that since I went through class one to class six primary in Togo, he would make me a deal by placing me in form two of the four years of middle school, and if I was catching up with my studies, he would let me write the common entrance exams as a shortcut to secondary school. By then, two of my brothers (Augustine and Paul), went to secondary school through that program and so I was happy to hear it.

The following day after the interview, I carried a chair and a table on my head to school. I secured a place at the back of the form two Classroom. With that, I began schooling again in my life. This time, I can tell you that my school was just a stone throw from my house. It was no more like walking quite some miles to school as compared to the one I went through in Togo. The environment too, was no longer like living in the middle of a thick forest.

Wusuta is a town that is under the Kpando District in the Volta Region of Ghana. Kpando District is believed to be one of the oldest administrative districts in Ghana dating back to the British colonial era. Wusuta is a low-income community which is faced with a growing incidence of poverty related social issues. One could mention problems such as family and chieftaincy disputes, early marriage of girls, divorces, child upbringing and property inheritance.

The inhabitants of Wusuta speak the Ewe language. The majority of them are Christians, while a cross-section of them are adherents of the traditional religion. Their major economic work is agriculture, hunting, and fishing. Some live-in houses, while others struggle to live in wooden-framed structures with grass-thatched roofing. Such structures cannot even withstand heavy rainfall.

In most cases, mud, bricks, cement blocks, leaf/thatch, wood, and burnt bricks are the essential materials that are used to construct walls of dwelling units. The main roofing materials are corrugated metal sheets. Few households have pipe-borne water as the main source of drinking water. Almost the whole township was using the river or the stream as the main source of drinking water (Dzigba or Yorvuime). When it rains, that was the time some people also collected it for their households.

The town has pipe-borne water, but the water did not flow regularly due to lack of funds to purchase fuel for the generator in order to function. However, when any rich man dies in the town by then, the family members pay so that the pipe-borne water can flow. On that day, water will flow in my father's house since we have a pipe in our house. On occasions such as Christmas and New Year, the pipe-borne water flows as well.

The major economic activities of the people of Wusuta are subsistence farming and lake fishing. Women in particular buy fish and processed by indigenous traditional methods of drying, salting and smoking. The fish is marketed by water transportation. Community meeting is often held in the traditional chief's palace and public market square. There are two social and cultural dance groups at Wusuta noted as Dumas borborbor and Venononyo. Another term for borborbor is "Akpese." It is a circular dance with drumming. It is also part of our rich cultural heritage an entertainment on special occasions.

The kerosene lamp was the source of lighting in Wusuta community, and there was no electricity by then. Households used wood and charcoal as a form of fuel for cooking. As I am writing this book, I can boast of electricity extended to Wusuta and beyond. The use of child labor constituted another prominent issue of the time. This contributed to high child dependency as boys and girls from twelve to sixteen worked on the family farm as the means of supplementing family income.

The root causes of these were poverty, unemployment, and cultural practices. Some of these children were students, so what happened was that they either forgo education or combined work and schooling. These were some of the issues an African child had to go through as a means of training for adulthood. The conditions they worked under are hazardous, horrendous, in-humane yet they don't have a choice. These were some of the issues I was battling with as a young kid at the time I was in school at Wusuta.

When I got to form three in the first term, the head teacher encouraged me to try the common entrance examination, which I did. Surprisingly, when the result came in, I passed it. I got admission into my first choice of secondary school; Kpando Secondary School (Kpasec for short). The same secondary school my brother, Augustine Ankuvie attended. He was preparing to enter into the University of Ghana at Legon in Accra in Ghana to study medicine. At the same time, my brother Paul Ankuvie was in form three. Even though I passed the common entrance examination and was happy at one time, at another moment, I was sad due to financial problems.

A few days after the results were announced to the whole school at assembly, the head teacher called me to his office. He basically informed me that I could leave the school to join my parents in raising money toward my going to secondary school. I took his advice and left for Akposso Bibi, my father's cocoa farm. I arrived one afternoon, and everyone was wondering why I came to the village since school was still in progress.

I broke the news, and they all finally understood the reason why I had to come at that time. It was good news yet the money problem again! My brother Augustine was getting ready to enter into university for the first time to study medicine. Paul was also going to the third year of the five-year secondary course, and I was joining him in the same school to start my five-year secondary education.

You can foresee the financial burden on the shoulders of my parents. The following day, I resumed the usual farming work. I had to help my parents as we used to do when we were in primary school in Togo. By then, it was in early July 1988, and in September 1988, I had to report to Kpando Secondary School. Being the same school that my brother Paul attended, it means when he was going back to school, we had to go together.

Early in the morning when we woke up, we sharpened cutlass and set to weed my father's cocoa farm. He has a vast land of cocoa plantation that fetched him money to take care of us. However, he had so many mouths to feed and bills to pay. Let me tell you how cocoa is grown from the tree up to the table. It is a product that is mostly grown in West Africa. It grows very well in raining environments around the tropical zone by the equator.

Cocoa tree is therefore a tropical tree often with shades among other trees. It is a labor intensive, sensitive, and delicate. It requires a lot of a care. It is a small tree between three to eight meters tall. Some small-scale farmers plant in a row, making sure it is well spaced. When the tree is shaded by other forest trees, it can reach a height of ten to twelve meters. From the beginning, the process starts with seedlings and then later transplanted.

If my memory could serve me well, cocoa tree begins to bear fruits from its fourth to sixth year. It has a straight stem, and the leaves are large and glossy. Somewhere along the line, the color of the leaves become green at maturity stage. The fruit of the cocoa trees is inside its pod in the form of seeds. The fruits come about as a result of tiny and waxy pink clusters together on its trunk as well as the branches.

For the sake of those people who don't know, I will say that there are two harvesting seasons, one as minor and the other as the major. The minor season starts in between May and August and the main season is from September to March. The color of the fruit as it grows on the trunk and the branches is green, and maroon.

Some have an elongated shape and must ripen before being harvested. The harvesting of cocoa is done by removing the ripe pods from the tree to the ground and then collecting them into baskets or sacks. The fruits are harvested when they exhibit a yellow color with long handles or curved knives (knives that are mitten with steel tools). You can also use machetes to remove the ripe fruits that are closer to the ground.

The harvested pods are collected together, and a day is set for the breaking. This is done in order to gather enough manual labor since it is needed on the day the pods will be broken. Usually, the farmer uses his or her family members and couples with the immediate neighbors. One early morning, preferably Saturday, the pod-breaking operation begins. Foods and drinks will be provided to the people that are gathered to break the pod. As the farmers sit down in a circular form to break the pods, the fruits are removed into baskets or containers while the pod husk is thrown away. My father's pod-breaking operation could take four to five hours and about twenty pod breakers were solicited.

While the cocoa pod-breaking is taking place, we the children of my father and other village women carried the baskets full of the beans to a place where it shall be piled up. Whenever all the beans have been removed from the pods and piled up together, that is the moment you cover them with plantain branches or mats for quick fermentation to take place. The layers that are used to cover the beans heat it up and the seeds undergo what I will refer to as sweating and it enables the thick seeds to ferment.

The fermentation period is about one week. The purpose is to remove the bitter taste from the beans. As cocoa ripens, it tastes sweet like sugar and during the sweating stage, the sugar contents are converted into acid (bitter taste) and it must be removed. A perfect brown color is a signal that the beans are well-fermented and can be dried.

At the end of the fermentation process, the cocoa beans are now ready for drying. This is done to eliminate the moisture in the beans in the course of fermentation. In the village, the drying of the bean is simply done by spreading it either on the ground or on the table. We dried ours in the sun on bamboo trestles covered by mats. During the drying period, the beans are turned within short intervals for better aeration, and to also check beans that may be germinated.

The drying process normally takes two weeks in the village. Eventually, when the beans are dried, they are put or scooped into bags or sacks and carried to the buying agent for sale. These are the various processes of cocoa production from the tree to the buying agent. These are the farming activities I, my brothers, and sisters underwent in order to receive financial support from our father toward our education.

In the middle of August 1988, everything was confirmed that I will be going to my first choice of secondary school. I became happy because it is the same school my brother Augustine, who is now a medical doctor, attended and Paul was attending F3 (Secondary School form three). My parents prepared for us to set off to school. My mother in particular made us "gari," and "shitor" in addition to sugar, laundry, soaps, and other provisions as supplement for the dining hall's food. Gari is cassava-toasted granules. It is a staple food for West African nations. To make gari, you have to pay for the cassava to be grinded to little chunks by the machine or have it done manually. The next thing is to put the grinded cassava through a mesh. The purpose is to eliminate the big chunks out in order to get an almost powder. Right after that, you can then roast it in a big silver copper over fire. The roaster has to constantly sit by the fire and be stirring it to prevent it from burning. The end product is obtained as gari.

Shitor on the other hand, is a hot, spicy sauce that is made in Ghana and West Africa. Just like we have salsa as a sauce in Mexico, and ketchup in the United States, in Ghana too, we have a well, rich, dark, reddish-brown sauce called shitor. It is served with dishes like steamed rice, plantain, yam, rice with beans, etc. To make it, you need to combine chopped onions in vegetable oil, ginger powder, tiny shrimps, chicken stock, hot peppers, smoked herring, and tomato paste.

Cook these ingredients on a source of heat while frequently stirring it. The finished result should look like a dark, reddish-brown color and a thick texture in terms of color. You now have "shitor," ready to use. It is really spicy. You need to store it in a glass with a cover and ensure there is a little oil on top of the sauce. Students often carry it to school to eat with gari and kenkey.

I remembered that toward the ending of August, my brother Paul and I left Akposso-Bibi to Wusuta, our hometown for the final preparations. We got home late in that evening. The following day Sunday, I fetched water and washed the rest of my clothes. I neatly pressed them with a charcoal iron, folded all of them into a wooden chop box, and locked it with padlock. Other few required school kits were put in a medium handbag, except my school uniform. In the first week of September, we were en route to Kpando Secondary School.

By eight o'clock in the morning, Paul and I arrived at school. The vehicle made a stop at the front gate of the school.

I saw the big sign board that read Kpando Secondary School. When we alighted, my brother carried his heavy handbag, and I carried my box on my head while the other luggage was in my hand following him.

At the time we approached the administration block of the school, I overheard some students shouting the word "Nino-Nino." It is a term that is used for the first arrival like me by then. That is to say, all the first-year students were nicknamed "Nino'. Students who were in the fifth year (Form Five, O-Level Candidates) and those who were in Upper Six Form (A-Level students) were pretty much the seniors. They were the bullies in the school.

The school has a boarding and day system. It is the system that puts all the students from the various ethnic groups under one umbrella. Accommodation is provided for us and if your parents cannot afford the boarding fees, you have to be a day student. You are forced to make friends without asking of his or her tribe. As you begin Form One, with the boarding system you will become used to it and tolerate one another without a question. There are many boarding schools in Ghana.

When the first-year students reported to school for the first time, the seniors who already reported would begin bullying them. That very day, my first appearance became horrible. Some seniors out of their free will, offered to assist me with my baggage. I did not know that I was going to pay for that kindness from the bullies. Even though my brother, Paul was walking with me, he could not do anything to remedy the situation. He was in Form Three, while the bullies were in Form Five and Sixth Form, far ahead of him.

The school is divided into five houses with a teacher as housemaster or headmistress. I found my name in house five, while my brother was in house one. There were daily routines to follow as a boarder, and that was the case in

Kpando Secondary School. The tasks were distributed evenly among all the five houses, supervised by its house leaders known as house captains. Early in the morning, by five a.m., the school bell would ring for us to wake up. By then, it was the British system of education and as such, the student body was divided into two groups, notably form 1-5, followed by the lower and upper sixth form.

Admission into the school was through the Common Entrance Examination. When you pass it, your grades were sent to your first choice of secondary school and you are picked by the headmaster or headmistress. The processes were put in place in order to eliminate some candidates because of limited accommodation issue. As I was saying, bullying and other victimization were the order of the day. I suffered from body harm as a result of school yard bullying. Some were in the form of kneeling down on your knees, sexual harassment on the parts of girls, pulling of nose, mimicking of your last name, and nicknaming. I Guessed I was nineteen years old when I entered into Secondary School and by then I thought that was a factor to the bullying.

Life on the campus was easy for the form five and upper sixth students as seniors, while we the first-year students found it difficult. A typical example was that every upper sixth student had a servant from the first-year students. What it means is that you the first-year student will be required to collect water for a sixth-former, wash his or her clothes, and even bring him or her food from the dining hall every day until the day he or she graduates. That includes breakfast, lunch and dinner. So, while you are going to the dining hall, you have to carry his or her plate along with you. You will see almost every first-year student carrying a rubber bag to the dining hall. This bag contained your senior man's plate in addition to your own. My good friend Emmanuel Gavua and I were always carrying rubber bag containing plates.

Mr. Edwin became my senior man. He was popularly known as "Bolingo." I became his servant until he graduated from the school. Form One students were responsible for sweeping the dormitories, classrooms, and school compounds. During the weekend, we had to scrub the bathroom and the smelly toilet. That has been the tradition in the Ghanaian Secondary schools. I am sure it is still going on today under the new educational reform. Senior Secondary School (SSS). We attended the headmaster's assembly every Monday. It is then followed by the senior housemaster and the master on duty.

The senior prefect (SP) most of the time, announced the name of seniors on duty for the week, after which we rushed to classroom for lessons to start. The boarders ate three square meals every day namely breakfast, lunch, and dinner. We had rice water porridge (Koko) and roasted maize porridge (Tom-Brown) alternatively. Lunch was rice with beans, rice with stew, and plantains. Gari (roasted cassava granules) comes with beans. Dinner was made up with either groundnut soup or palm nut soup with banku or rice balls. Sometimes the meals served to us during lunch and dinner was almost the same except that they are rotated.

My school did not have pipe-borne water flowing everywhere at that moment. There were few boreholes. I could recollect we had one for the boys and the other for the girls. We had one big water storage facility near the kitchen that collected the rainwater. Students in F1-3 were often asked to fetch water from the boreholes for the kitchen use. We were driven from the classroom to do so for a few hours which disrupted class hours. Whenever this type of situation happened, the master on duty and the seniors become busy while other teachers sat under one particular mango tree engaging in conversation.

If you were not satisfied with the dining hall's food, you had to go to the private venders (Amawe base) behind house two dormitories to eat. But make sure you are not caught during class hours. Students who had gari and shitor ate their food in the dormitory, while the poor ones from the villages whose food finished in no time just look on stirring in the air for nothing really. You may have gari but no shitor nor sugar, and you have to look for someone who has it for partnership. When you are lucky to get someone and you guys are eating together, anybody who approached to join was not allowed. We called it (NCNC), meaning no contribution no chop. Simply means if you don't bring anything, you will not be allowed to eat in the group.

Kpando Secondary School is one of the most respected Schools in the Volta Region of Ghana. Discipline was in its highest level in those days when I got admission into the first year. There was no room for tales of disobedience, drugs, laziness, etc. You were either rewarded for good behavior or punished severely. A student could be withdrawn if his or her behavior was not conducive for the school's environment. Simply put, there was no babysitting issue. As I mentioned earlier on, we had a wake-up call. That is, the bell was rung exactly at five o'clock for the students to get up from bed. If you dare to ignore it, seniors on duty would lash you with a belt as they went around making sure that we were all awake. Some seniors did not care to wet you with cold water should you decide to be sleeping in bed while you were supposed to be up.

Imagine how you used to sleep relaxingly in your home and wake up whenever you wanted. The day you set your foot into that boarding house, from that time onward, you could no longer do anything at your own discretion. You cannot be late to any school gathering. The same way when classes begin, you better be there waiting for your teacher. If you failed to go through your teacher's previous lesson before coming to class, you should better be standing by. We paid close attention in class while the teacher was teaching. In case you were caught looking around by your teacher, you could kneel down on your knees for the rest of your teacher's lesson period.

Those days, there was nothing like video games to play, unlike it is today. You better do what you were told by seniors. Misbehaviors of a certain nature were instantly met with cane from dynamic Senior Housemaster of the school. His disciplinary measures were second to none. The message was clear, respect for elders. Every adult could discipline you at any time without any hesitation. You did not dare to look at an elder's face when he or she was addressing you.

You had to even keep your hand at your back while you were being talked to. What do we see today? Junior students put their hands in their pockets or might be looking at your face scornfully. The juniors were supposed to assist elders by carrying their belongings whenever they come across them during my time. A senior student could ask you the junior to get up so that he or she can have your place. These were some of the measures that were geared toward the realization of good behaviors and sound academic life.

Looking back, I can proudly state that some situations were tough yet today, those disciplinary measures have made significant impacts on my life. Boarding school discipline had contributed immensely to my present well-being. I have acquired self-esteem, skills, getting along easily with people of a different race, and religious tolerance. As I am writing this book, I hold a Bachelor of Science in Business Administration with the concentration in Business Management with the help of self-discipline dated back in Kpando Secondary

School in Ghana. "Charity begins at home," so goes the old adage. Furthermore, "Spare the rod and spoil the child."

We the first-year students suffered from bulling as well as other forms of discipline. A group of senior students would just provoke you for no reason. The bullies could even get your face smashed, taunted or brushed. They claimed to have endured such or similar ordeals. Their violent acts of behaviors scared some of us. I felt we did not deserve to be treated like that but who was I going to complain to?

Bullying in my secondary school was as well in the form of stealing of the first-year students' provisions that they brought from home to supplement the dining hall's food. Bullies forced the first-year victims to open their chop box. Right in your presence, whatever they wished to take could be taken without a word. I could remember that three of us were stopped on our way to evening studies (prep), taken to a F3A or B classroom, and lined up in front of the whole students to dance. My friend Emmanuel and I in addition to another one suffered on that faithful day. It was mockery, and shameful act. We were asked to entertain the class by a cross section of bullies in that particular class. One of them was demonstrating for us to emulate. They were laughing at us while the three of us were busily dancing. We had to comply otherwise we were not going to be released any time soon.

You could be subjected to teasing, taunting, hitting, nose pulling, threatening and many more. Any sign of insubordination during the time of bullying was met with more severe physical punishment. Such behaviors made some of the first-year students to be socially isolated. Bullying continued until all first-year students were officially welcomed to the school through a ceremony known as Nino's Night. It was a welcoming event organized to usher the first-year students into the school. After Nino's Night, the first-year students are therefore known as "Kpasecans," meaning official students of Kpando Secondary School.

Bullying also ceased to stop from that day. It was done before the whole student body closed down for Christmas holiday. The ceremony to usher or welcome the first-year students of Kpando Secondary School was organized by the Entertainment Department of the school. The ceremony was held on Saturday night as part of entertainment activity. The first-year students were taught a series activity ahead of this occasion. One senior bully in form five volunteered to teach us all the activities that were required of us on that bitter day. I personally felt it was a horrible day set aside to inflict all the disgraceful behaviors of the bullies on the innocent first year students.

There was a rumor that once that was done no senior could bully a first-year student. But that was not the case. When you were caught loitering in the dormitory of senior students, you should be ready to face more bullying. On this day, all the first-year students were baptized with the smelly gari mixtures. It was held in early December before the whole students break for the Christmas holiday. We were taught stupid songs and some poems to recite. Other funny activities to make the whole student body laugh were equally incorporated into it. We were forced to wear torn shirts over a pair of trousers.

We dressed up as creatures. They painted our faces with colors as well as other decorations. The bottom line was that we were the subject of ridicules on that day. Some of us too were blindfolded. We sang songs composed by our so-called teacher bully, Bengay. One particular song was composed as the anthem of the school concerning us, the first-year students. I could only remember the first line. (We are the ninos of Kpasec...). Basically, we are the first-year student of the school...bla...bla... The night stayed up late because we were about one hundred and over students in the first year.

The climax of the ceremony came where we were lined up one by one, blindfolded, ready to be baptized on stage. When it reached your turn, they would remove your blindfold, after which you had to mention your name, age, hometown, and of course, your nickname given to you aloud. This information was on the placard which you were wearing. For example, I was nicknamed "Mu-shu-mu-du." I did not even know the meaning of that. It might be meaning something stupid or demeaning. Other sister secondary schools like Kpando Technical and Bishop Herman Secondary students even conveyed to our campus so as to witness this event.

We walked to the stage, and they brushed your face pulled your nose a couple of times, then poured the smelly gari mixtures on your head and all over your body. After the ceremony, the attire worn cannot be used again. You have to discard it. We were then known as Kpasecans, meaning we are officially welcome and are now part and parcel of the school. When the ceremony was over, we ran to our hostel to get a quick bath and returned to clean the dining hall and rearrange it for church service on the following day.

It was mandatory for all the students in secondary school to attend a daily devotional service. In Ghana, the constitution provides for freedom of region. Public schools are either day or boarding schools. These schools were first established by the Christian missionaries. Some of them were the Portuguese, British, Dutch, and German, just to mention a few. Somewhere along the line during the colonial era, the Ghana government became a co-sponsor of these mission schools and finally took over them in order to ensure a national standard.

In some of these schools, even after the government took over, the devotional leadership was still in the hands of a member of the same faith of the school. Kpando Secondary was therefore an evangelical Presbyterian school with a priest as a religious leader. During the Christian service moments, we had to recite the Lord's Prayer, followed by a Bible reading and a blessing. Those of us who were residing in the boarding house were required to attend a nondenominational church service on every Sunday.

As members of the Roman Catholic Church, we attended church services at Kpando Technical School. The school was just a stone throw from ours. Students could wear a decent kaki trouser and a nice, white shirt on top to church services. We were also allowed to wear "kente" cloth to church services. "Kente" cloth is a Ghanaian native or traditional cloth that is usually worn by royals and rich people during very important social, as well as religious, occasions. This cloth is woven in Ashanti and the Volta Region of Ghana. "Kente" cloth is worn by wrapping it around the body and dragging it over the shoulders. The strips of the cloth must be straight, horizontally and vertically. The bottom of the cloth must hang at the same length all the way around the wearer's ankles.

We the Ghanaians like to fellowship at church service by dancing and praising Almighty God. Religion hence plays a vital role in our lives. During praise and worship time, the whole congregation sings, dances, and offer prayers. We even dance during offering time. I really cherished this aspect very well. That is when the congregation leaves their pews row by row and dances the aisles in order to drop their collections, usually in woven baskets. Despite the fact that students come from the various ethnic backgrounds and speak different languages, everyone becomes unified under one universal God on Sundays during worship.

The general atmosphere at Kpando Secondary was conducive for academic life. As a boarder, we were always on campus and cannot go out freely unless you ask a written permission through your house captain and it is authorized by your house master. Your housemaster's authorization permits you to go out to the township and returned as instructed. To travel outside the school, your request must be signed finally by the school's senior housemaster. When you were found in Kpando town by any master of the school without a written authorization as a boarder, you were immediately asked to return to campus and report yourself to the appropriate house captain or housemaster for disciplinary action.

I can still remember how the five of us were caught by our housemaster on one Saturday afternoon in town, trying to have a good time without permission. We thought we were avoiding him by passing through unexpected routes. All of sudden, we just ran into him. There was no way we could escape from him. Have you ever been into any situation like that where you did not want someone to see you but eventually have to be seen? That was exactly what happened to us. We knew he was always hanging in town arresting students, yet we took the risk to also go out unduly.

You can guess what happened to us. As soon as he saw us, he asked us to come to where he was sitting. If my memories can serve me well, he was sitting down, waiting to board a vehicle that was loading passengers to travel outside Kpando town. He requested to see our written permission, which we could not produce. He also mentioned how he knew we did not have it. He also mentioned how he knew that some students have been going to town without permission as a boarder.

He sent us to report ourselves to our house captain (a senior student in final year, A-level). We quickly returned to campus and reported ourselves to our house captain, awaiting his return from his trip. He at long last came back on Sunday night and sent for us to come to his bungalow.

There, we faced his wrath. He spoke about how he has been timing us to fall in his trap. Luckily for him, he got us on that faithful day. He punished all of us for three to four days with hard labor. When we closed from classes, we had to fetch our buckets to collect some gravel to his pig's den.

Other campus lifestyles also got some of us frustrated and I wished I could have done the same, yet I did not get the opportunity. By then, some of the boarders on campus came from very rich and well to do families. They brought expensive clothes, foods, and exorbitant footwear to school to show off. Some of them left the house for school and that was the chance to get away from their parents, hence the golden opportunity to show off extravagant lifestyles instead of being there for their studies. You could see that they were not prepared to study even though they had the higher marks for passing common entrance examination. During evening study period, you would find them sitting near beautiful girlfriends engaged in conversation.

Sporting activities were great moments of jubilation for us in those days at Kpasec. That is the time we used to have a little bit of break from the long classroom hours and other frustrations. We usually had inter-house athletic game competition followed by inter-school competition. During the interschool competition, all the secondary schools that were classified in one zone conveyed to one school as a venue so as to compete among themselves for the various field and track events. My school, Kpasec for short, used to emerge as the overall winner or winning majority of events at the end of this sporting event. The sporting activities sometimes lasted two weeks or more. Kpando Technical School was often chosen as the venue. Students sang songs called "Dza-ma" in order to cheer their winning teams. (Yebesi dza-ma ooo, kpasecfoe besi dza-ma ooo). The winning school was awarded a trophy and my school Kpasec students, often had a misunderstanding with Kpantec students which resulted in a physical fight. For some weeks after the sporting activities, both school students were at a loggerhead.

As boarding students, at the weekends, family members were there to visit their sons and daughters. They brought them all the way from Accra and near prepared food and other provisions in order to supplement dining hall food. Those of us who came from a poor family where our parents and guardians have to struggle hard so as to get us school fees and transportation back to school, were disturbed with the expensive lifestyles of the well to do ones. Such was the case of we the middle-class students.

We did not have any frequent family members visit, let alone talk about bringing us food. The only time someone came was to announce you the death of a loved one. My brother Paul and I had to endure the pain of hardship on campus. Missing dinning hall's food was not an option. In the middle of these, Paul and I managed to get through even though we wished we had everything in school as some fortunate ones had. But there are consequences to having everything and not studying your books.

If you are nice and know what you are about in life, you will come across people and naturally, you could become friends. I humbled myself in school, focused my attention day in, day out for the reason why I had to be there, and before I realized I was in the company of similar students. I spoke of the five of us getting caught earlier on. This was how we came together as friends. Whenever these guys came back from vacation, some of them brought their food, including mine and together we kept them in my wooden chop box. We had smoked fish, kobi, mumuni, Keta school boys, gari, sugar, and Almighty shitor, very hot one of course. At our leisure time, we gathered and ate food from one bowl, a typical sign of brotherhood.

We ground fresh pepper in our hostel and used it to eat gari, Eba (the end result of pouring hot water on gari), and banku. I had the grinding equipment (Evegba or kole). In the middle of the hardships of the time, we persevered. My background always reminded me of my behavior at school and wherever I went to. I was, therefore, eager to advance myself in school through strong zeal and self-determination. Imagine you are born from parents and guardians who did not get the chance to go to school yet are working tremendously to educate you.

As a boarder, we did not get everything as easily and comfortably as living at home. Time was very precious, and you have to be conscious of it at all time. Our dormitories were very big and filled to capacity. Some first-year students did not even have beds to sleep on and had to lay their mattresses on the cemented floor to sleep at the time I was in first year from 1987 to 1988. Some of us fought among ourselves for the floor so as to sleep during those days. You would be sleeping just to realize your pillow is gone. The seniors can come at any time and remove your pillow to your surprise and use it.

Students attended evening studies from seven p.m. to nine p.m. Evening devotion was held at the hostel, after which all lights went off until early in the morning at five o'clock when the bell goes for us to wake up. You have to rush to the hostel after evening studies to eat food from your box before the bell goes for devotion because, after devotion, you must jump into your bed to sleep. If you are caught doing anything after ten p.m., you would receive some lashes from the seniors on duty by then. There was no mercy at all.

So far from my observation in the United States of America, I realized that everything is spoon-fed to the people living in terms of opportunities and facilities. What I mean is that life is easy as a result of the State of Union. Back in

Ghana, that was not the case. You have to work hard for everything because there is no State of Union working among African nations unlike the United States of America. This makes it for you to be extra vigilant. Life is not all that grim. Even though I got a Scholarship from Ghana Cocoa board to finance my education right from the third term of my first year up to form five, I still had to face the reality of the time. We usually go through three school terms and break for the long vacation in May or June.

School reopened either in the first or second week of September. The old British system of education by then required us to study a lot of subjects from form one to the third term of form three. Some of the subjects that were taught in those days were Geography, Mathematics, Additional Mathematics, English Language, English Literature, French Language, History, Agricultural Science, Accounting, Commerce, Bible Studies, Introduction to Business Management (IMB), Typewriting, and Home Science, just to mention a few.

Students in F1 to F3 studied a bunch of these subjects until the third term of form three, after which they have to choose eight subjects. These eight subjects are made up of three core and five electives. The core subjects are English Language, Mathematics, and a science subject. The Science subjects can either be General Science or Agricultural Science. General Science is sub-divided into Biology, Chemistry, and Physics. You will start studying these eight subjects right from form four to form five. You will then write a final exam which is administered by the West African Examination Council (WAEC) at the end of your fifth year which was popularly called O-Level.

Right from form one, there was a continuous assessment followed by midterm exams. The continuous assessment was composed of assignments, constant attendance, quizzes, and other classroom presentations. The midterm exam was made up of both objective and a written comprehension in the form of essay. This essay type of questions lasted approximately three hours. In the essay type of questions, your teacher expected you to exactly memorize the classroom notes and lessons taught and reproduce it the same manner he or she taught you. We the students, called it "Chew and pour" meaning reproducing lessons word for word.

When you take the comprehension text, you must demonstrate a strong sense of subject matter and a logical presentation of material fact. The midterm exam was graded on seventy percent while the continuous assessment covered the rest of thirty percent all making one hundred percent. Your grades were put on a terminal report card and posted to your parents and guardians, including your next term school fees. When you pass the O-Level exams with a good aggregate in six subjects out of eight subjects offered, you were admitted into a two-year advanced course (A-Level). The advanced two-year course was made up of lower and upper six. When you are lucky to make it into the previous secondary school you did your F1 to F5, you are hailed and given the uttermost respect deserved to you. You were popularly addressed by the juniors as "Sweet Lower."

After selecting subjects in form three, my friend Emma and I found ourselves in the business classroom. I took business subjects in addition to the three core ones. My subject combinations were English Language, Mathematics, Agricultural Science, Principles of Accounting, Introduction to Business Management (IBM), Commerce, French Language, and Economics. At the end of O-Level (F5) in 1993, I sat for the final exam conducted by the West African Examination Council known as (WAEC).

When the results came, I got division one with a 23 aggregate and a pass in the English Language. The grading system in Ghanaian schools at that moment was downward, with one being the highest while nine was the lowest. If you happened to get a credit in any subject, you were through to the next level. However, if you score a pass in a subject, you have to retake it again before you can move on to the next level of your education. Students are therefore supposed to score credit and above credit in all the core subjects (English Language, Mathematics, General Science or Agricultural Science) in order to advance to six Form (A-Level).

I realized that I could not go to Six Form as planned because I had a pass instead of a credit in English Language. I basically failed the English Language, a serious, disgraceful set back in my life. I became annoyed of myself but there was nothing I could do to change it. That leads me to say that in life, there are certain things that will happened to you and the outcome may not be what you desired for. When such things occur to you, please accept the outcome in good faith and move on. No amount of lamentation can change it at that moment. Luckily, my friend, Emma, made it through to Six Form level. I had another friend by the name Confidence Bansah at that very time. He attended Vakpo Secondary School. Mr. Confidence later attended Peki Training College and became a classroom teacher. Somewhere along the line, he received a calling and went to Trinity Theological Seminary in Accra. As I was writing this book, Mr. Confidence became an ordained Pastor in E.P Church glory to God. His status changed and became known as Rev. Confidence Bansah in Evangelical Presbyterian Church in Ghana. He was once attached to Medina E.P Church as District Pastor. Mr. Emma too got a job at Pepsi Cola Company in Accra at that time. As friends, we were all struggling those days. Praise Lord!

A pass in English Language caused me a downfall and that was when all my frustrations set in. I needed a difference of one mark from a pass to a credit. I had to register for the next year's exams so as to retake a minimum of six subjects. Remember that I took the exams in 1993, and 1994 was going to be the last secondary school set of O-Level and A-Level. That was the British traditional system of education in Ghana by then and a new Educational Reform was about to begin (Senior Secondary School (SSS).

Earlier on, while I was awaiting the O-Level exam results, I left as usual to the village in Togo. By then, my brother, Paul had also finished his A-Level courses at Ho Mawuli Secondary School in the Volta Region. We decided to raise some money in advance toward our exam results. In view of that, we planned to do a palm wine tapping business. By the time I got to the village, he already paid some laborers to fell the palm trees. Sixty trees were felled for the intended business. Palm wine tapping is an income-generating activity which is done in West Africa.

It is very dirty, tedious, and difficult job. It is not a pleasant job to do at all. You can easily get bruises from the rough nature of the palm trees. The wine from the palm is white and milky. It tastes sweet and it is collected from the palm tree. When you fell the palm tree, you have to ensure that the crown of the tree is well-exposed to enable the sap to be collected. My brother was doing the palm wine tapping while I was going round to collect the wine individually as well as firing them by the sunset.

Felling the palm tree is done manually by digging gradually around its roots and, with time, the tree would be on the ground. You then allow the felled palm trees, for two or three weeks, to ferment before you begin the tapping. The next thing you needed to do would be to remove its cover and bore a hole in it. At this stage, you need to set a small pot beneath the palm tree. Every morning, you have to go round with a big pot or jar to gather the wine from each tree. Mostly, one person did the collection while another one did the tapping. Right after the palm wine was collected in the morning, the one in charge of tapping went with a short, sharpened machete to cut a thin layer to facilitate easy flowing of the juice into the small pot beneath it.

Due to the time-consuming nature of palm wine tapping, you have to wake up early in the morning to begin it. So as soon as I woke up in the morning, I jumped into my farm or bush attire and set off with a big jar or gallon so as to collect the palm wine from the individual trees into the jar I was carrying. When the jar was full, I then proceeded to pour the wine into the stationary bigger pots and jars. In the first few days that you begin the tapping, you don't fire the palm trees.

After collecting the palm wine and we supplied it to our regular customers for sale, then I begin to make bundles of dried palm branches, which will be used later to fire the palm trees. At two to three o'clock in the afternoon, my brother and I would start firing the palm trees. We used straw to blow air into the bundle of dried branches that is used to fire the region of the palm trees. The short, sharpened machete is used again to cut thin layers of the region fired, and the trees are covered back and that does it for that day until the next morning.

Palm wine is very sweet when it is unfermented and begins to taste sour when the fermentation process sets in. It becomes vinegary when it is well-fermented for over a week or more. Some people like it when it tastes vinegary. To do the firing quickly, I have to drink a few calabashes of the well-fermented wine. When you are under the influence of the fermented palm wine, you can get the job done easily and happily. Throughout West Africa, palm wine is used to pour libations to the lesser gods on the ground. You always have to pour a few drops of palm wine on the ground before you drink it. It is a sign of showing appreciation and respect to the lesser gods. It is also drunk during traditional celebrations such as birthdays, funerals and marriage ceremonies.

It is part of Ghanaian culture to pour a few drops of drink on the ground before you go ahead to drink it. My brother and I also distilled some of the palm wine to make a local alcoholic drink which is known as "Akpeteshie." So, while we were selling the fresh palm wine, we were also distilling it. Some people call it "Agogro," "Sodabe," or "Apio." The wine must be fermented in barrels for a period of two weeks. You then pour a fermented wine into a tank and ensure that it is sealed. Apply heat underneath the tank for one and half hours.

Before you start applying the heat, you need to connect a copper pipe in the other opening of the same tank. As soon as the wine reached in boiling point, the supposed evaporated wine passes through the copper and as it reaches the part of the pipe that is in vast water-cooling bath, it creates a strong alcoholic drink that is collected into big bottle which is locally referred to as "Adzafi." The drink that comes out in the first ten minutes is so strong that nobody drinks it (this stage is called spirit). That one is reserved to dilute the weaker drink.

While we were distilling, my brother, Paul, often carried his single gun and walked few miles around to hunt for animals and birds. We cooked those birds (guinea fowls," Vetekle"), applied hot spices, and smoked them. We drank either palm wine or "Akpeteshie" and enjoyed their meat. Also, we went out to fish in the flowing river to catch some fishes without taking any precaution of the river. Despite the fact that the job was rough and tedious, we had fun with it as well as raised some money out of it for our educational needs.

Did you remember I went through this job to raise money for advanced level courses? I got my share of the money we raised and came back to campus just to realize I did not qualify for my long-awaited post-secondary course.

The reason was obvious; I had a pass in the English Language instead of a credit. What a disappointment! My frustrations all started to set in. I had to retake the O-Level exam again.

At that time, the new educational reform was about to be implemented and O-Level candidates had only one more chance to sit for their exams. All candidates who needed to retake the exam had to register. I felt disgraced and could not see my mates wearing their new uniform for A-Level while I had to register to retake the exam in the same environment. I quickly cancelled the idea of registering in Kpando Secondary in order to retake the last O-Level exam.

I left Kpando Secondary and started looking for other secondary schools for registration. I first went to Anfoega Secondary school to consult the headmaster, but that was not possible. I proceeded to Vakpo Secondary School too, just to be told there was no vacancy. That was in 1994, the last opportunity for O-Level candidates. As a result, the headmasters were using the occasion to receive briberies before a student was duly registered. Bribery and corruption are some of the social vices in Ghanaian society.

Being a young guy trying to consult the headmasters for re-registration does not work well in Ghana. If you are accompanied by an elderly person to see the headmaster of a school behind a closed door that will rather yield a positive result. Furthermore, I gathered courage and went to Agate Secondary School and could not get admission as well. I knew that the head teachers were looking for cola. Unfortunately for me, the money I had was not enough to spare some for cola (bribery and corruption).

At this juncture, I returned to Hohoe, where my brother Moses Ankuvie, was staying. I started helping him in his Lotto Business by then and at the same time, was thinking of how to resume my desperate search for more secondary schools in order to register. During the few days that I spent in his Lotto

Kiosk, the idea came to me to share some thoughts with a female formal secondary school friend by the name of Diana. The two of us had just finished Kpasec and she got admission to St. Teresa's Teacher Training College and was getting ready to report to school.

While we were attending school at Kpasec, in the holidays, the two of us walked a few miles to HEPS, Hohoe Evangelical Presbyterian Secondary School, at Hohoe for extra classes. Owing to that, I was not a stranger in their house. I know her father popularly known as "Ofa." He was by then one of the sales agents at a filling station. I told Diana about my inability to get a school to register for the last O-Level exam. I also lamented to her how I was going to return to my father's cocoa farm in the village for the last resort. My father told me to reach out to extended family members for financial help and if I could not get a school to register, I should return to the land. I discussed with my friend how I tried a few schools and did not get any opportunity to register because all the secondary schools I had visited earlier on were all filled up.

The lady expressed her dissatisfaction about my situation and promised me to talk to her father (Ofa) for any possible assistance. According to my savior her father knew the headmasters of some secondary schools in the Hohoe area. She also stated that the trucks of some schools used to come to the filling station where her father was working at. The following day, Diana's father stopped over by my brother's Lotto kiosk. He told me that her daughter briefly informed him that I needed help. That was why he decided to come and asked me about my desperate situation.

Even though I was ashamed of my situation, I had to explain it to him. He assured me that he would accompany me to Likpe Secondary School to see the headmaster so that I can get a chance to retake the subjects I needed. We set up a day together to meet. The day eventually came, and we went to Likpe Mate Secondary School as planned. When we got to the administration block of the school, we saw a lot of students who were in the same predicament with me trying to get a final opportunity to register so that they can retake the supposed final O-Level exam. A huge crowd of students, of course!

Ofa mentioned my name, Komla, and said we have a problem, but I should have faith in God. He was leading the way among the huge crowd of students and asked me to follow him. Seeing the big number of students, my frustration grew. When we got to the entrance of the headmaster's office, he requested to see the headmaster. He was told by a messenger that the headmaster could not be seen simply because he was very busy. He then sent the messenger to the head with a name on a piece of paper that was known to the two of them.

Ofa said to me that when that note is handed to him and he read it, no matter how busy he was, he was sure that there would be a positive answer coming out from the headmaster to him. Luckily and miraculously, the messenger came back and without any hesitation, he was allowed to consult the headmaster while I was waiting among the crowded students. While I was waiting, I overhead a big laughter in the office and within a few minutes, the messenger came and called me, and I followed him to the office.

The headmaster requested to see my grades from Kpando Secondary School. He made a comment that my grades were not bad at all. As such, he will give me the last chance to retake it. All my particulars were taken and the required amount of money for the registration was paid, and receipt was also issued to me signifying the end of the deal.

Ofa and the headmaster shook hands, and we left his office. What a joy and surprise in my heart! What a miracle had just happened? According to Ofa, the two of them had a good discussion behind closed door and I felt it. I could not believe my eyes having seen the huge crowd of students waiting outside for their turn to see the headmaster. I was wondering about whatever went on behind closed door on that faithful day. You can also imagine it for yourself. Maybe whenever you and I meet one day somewhere it will be then that I can tell you.

You can see how God can use other people to help the needy in society? You can have a father and mother, brothers and sisters, uncles and you just name them, there will be a time in your life when you will need a help, but your own relatives may not be there to assist you. But God will place other people on your desperate way to offer you a helping hand. Are you now beginning to understand me? This should send you a signal that whatever your situation is, don't just give up asking for help. There is a God out there that is watching and can see from everywhere and will never forsake you.

Dear reader of this book, I want to let you know that it is very good to know people in life. The mere fact that my friend and I got to know each other back in Secondary School from 1988-1993, I benefited from that in 1994. Listen to my piece of advice; in whichever way you think you can be of a help to someone in need in life, please don't hesitate to do so. The reward for that may not come instantly but it will eventually come. If you like, do not even think of any reward before helping the needy in life. I believe your greatest reward await you at the right time. Almighty God, the Alpha and Omega, the beginning and the end, will never forsake you but, you will be rewarded abundantly at the appropriate time.

Even though it is good to help people, you need to be aware of the ungrateful ones. They are the ones pretending to love you. They actually don't love you, but rather want to use you to get to their destination. They looked like Christians and dressed gorgeously to churches. They appeared to be nice and friendly in front of everyone yet are full of hidden human behaviors from sight. Their pay back often leads to grief and betrayal. You will therefore see their true colors when you are no longer useful to them. They are the ungrateful and unthankful ones. While you are leading them to cross the river, they will be insulting the mouth of the crocodile even though they have not yet finished crossing the water.

Ofa and I boarded a taxi back to Hohoe. He was the one who even paid my transportation fees from Hohoe to Likpe and from Likpe back to Hohoe. May God richly bless him. My brother, Moses let me stay with him From November 1993 till May and June 1994. By then, he had one bedroom and a small verandah. I was living with him, his wife and their first-born baby boy, Mawuli. We watched television and ate food as well on the verandah in the daytime. When it was time to go to bed, I had to put the couch on each other and lay a small mattress on the carpet to sleep.

Early in the morning, I have to wake up because everyone else in the bedroom had to come out through the verandah. Life was not comfortable, but I had to manage it in good faith. When I woke up in the morning while I was with my brother, I had to put away the mattress and re-arrange the couches in order. We were living in a big compound house with some other tenants. The caretaker apportioned part of the compound to all the tenants in the house to sweep every morning. As soon as I joined my brother and his wife, I took her regular portion.

I swept it and cleaned our kitchen every morning. I also helped her carried a heavy provisions wooden box for my brother's wife to Hohoe trotro lorry station, where she usually goes to sell them. By nine o'clock in the morning, I would take a shower and off to my brother's Lotto kiosk in order to assist him make a sale. Most of the time, he was gone on his bike while I was left alone with a lot of angry customers to deal with.

In the afternoon, around three to four o'clock, I have to go to the wife at the lorry station to find out of dinner after which I will proceed to the public market to buy the necessary ingredients. When I finished making dinner, then I quickly hurried up to my remedial studies. Most of the time, I was late for the classes. I could tell from my teacher's eyes that he was not happy with me. At the same time, there was nothing I could do about it. That was the situation in which I was until it was time for me to go to Likpe to retake the O-Level exam.

May and June 1994 finally came for the last opportunity to re-write the last O-Level exams in school setting. Ofa gave me some pocket money to use for my transportation as well as food. I arrived, took the exams and spent two weeks at Likpe Secondary School. After the exams, one morning, I returned to Hohoe. When the results came out, this time I made it in English Language. Come and see how happy I was!! The one-mark difference made me to almost go crazy and after one year everything became normal.

I don't know how to thank Almighty God for using Diana, my good friend and the father as a source of help at a time when I actually needed assistance but no one from my own family was in position to assist me. All Ofa's efforts were generously rewarded. He was also happy and congratulated me. His kindly gestures were few. This time, even though I got all requirements for A-Level, because of money issue and lack of interest, I changed my mind to rather go to Teacher Training College. The training college students were by then enjoying allowances, something that can benefit me to go through the system, unlike A-Level courses. As a result, a lot of students were applying for admission.

Dear reader of this book, I need you to do me a favor. I want to plead with you to extend your kindly feelings toward people whom you may come across in life. Try to have human compassion for mankind in need. That is just one of the reasons why I am writing this book. In life, I am sure you will agree with me that bad things happen to good people. Whenever I come back from work in the U.S. and I sit on the couch, my mind travels back to my roots. I think of how I got to the America, and it always seems to me as a miracle. For a son of a cocoa farmer born and raised in the middle of a cocoa farm with no family member in America, but is now living in USA, I found it very miraculous.

I don't get it, but it is real. I feel it is beyond human understanding. I believe it is like "Man proposes, and God disposes." It does not pay to be kind and generous. The lesson I learned from my situation is that, in life, when everything seems not to be working for you, don't just give up. Continue to endure and hang in there. It is a stage in life. Sometimes, when you think of how you have to use your money, time, and energy to assist someone you barely know, it hurts. Is it not? However, doing so for the sake of God is rewarding at the right time.

When I was young growing up, I used to observe my parents and guardians closely. They seemed to be concerned about other people more than us, their own children in the house. I did not understand it by then. Looking back in retrospect, I can now understand why I met people who helped me without even knowing my parents. I am therefore, of the view that the outcome of helping the needy is far more rewarding than how much it will cost you to give out.

Mark it on the wall that your own parents, guardians, etc. and what have you not would all be still alive, yet at a point in time, you may encounter a problem. Even though they are around, you may not get the instant help from them. By the time they come to rescue you, your situation or condition may or might worsen. The chance or opportunity can slip away and may not come back.

Don't also forget where to pass to climb a tree in order to get to the top of it. Most people who have been given help turn to stab the back of the very person who has given them that assistance. I don't think it is a good or smart thing to do. God in heaven will pay you back when you decide to do so. This type of selfish behavior makes them fall from tall buildings and land to marketplace. It is like from grace to grass.

Humbling yourself can cause you to be successful in life. Your character coupled with your integrity can enable you to rise up in the face of adversity. Obstacles or impediments may come your way to the extent that you could be at the point of breaking. But try as much as possible to hold on unto it. A better day is about to come. When it does, you will even forget about your bad moment. Henceforth, your future is based on the mistakes of the past. All your difficult moments of the past are to strengthen you for better future.

Personally, anybody who has done something good for you at a point in life, you have to be thankful to him or her. A word of thanks would be appreciated. Some people are motivated and also have a desire to benefit from what they have offered in return. I think that you should offer a helping hand out of freewill.

Even in the Bible, I can recollect from Matthew 5:16 "Let your light so shine before men, that they may see your good works and glorify your Father in heaven." Allow God in heaven to use you as an instrument to touch the lives of other people in return of everlasting blessings. Be generous toward mankind. I don't mean you should let people have your last money, meal, etc. It can simply be in the form of emotional support or devoting much time to someone.

MY TEACHER TRAINING COLLEGE ERA

All said and done, I took the last O-Level exams in 1994 at Likpe-Mate and by the grace of God, I passed them. This time, I got the required grade in order to proceed with my academic life. Previously, I wanted to go to Six Form for Advanced Studies and then into university. That was my original plan. Since things did not go on the way I wanted it to be, so I thought it twice to rather go to Teacher Training College. If I have to do A-Level course, I was going to face financial difficulties.

By then, you have to buy a Teacher Training registration form, which was being sold at 5000 cedi (less than U.S. $1.00). My brother with whom I was staying at Hohoe was facing serious financial problems and as a result of that he could not provide me with this money. I remembered that I went to my mother at Anfoega Dzana, but she too claimed she did not have money to give me. Time was going against me. I needed money badly to buy the teacher training registration form. Our father was helpless at Wusuta. The village at Akposso, too, was very dry at that moment.

One morning, as usual, I was in my brother's Lotto kiosk and my good female friend passed by. We had a conversation and the issue of buying the form came in. Frankly speaking, I told her that I could not find money to buy the registration form. She left and informed her father again. The following day, her father brought me the 5000 old cedi. I shamefully extended my hands and collected it. I rode my brother's bike to St. Francis Training College at Hohoe and finally bought the registration form for Teacher Training College. When Diana's father gave me the money this time, he told me something that I will never forget in my life.

He told me that I was the eleventh persons he came across in life that needed help desperately. The ten previous people he helped earlier in life all forgot about him. None of them came to say thank you at least or to express his or her sincere gratitude to him so I should be aware of it. I became disturbed but moved by his words. Also, his message encouraged me to climb as much ladder as I can so that I can be in position to give back one day. I put all my thoughts in prayers and promised not to let myself down. To me personally, I owe him, and I have to do everything possible to pay back.

I filled the registration form and chose the only French Teacher's College in Ghana by the name of Mount Mary Training College. It is called L'Ecole Normale de Somanya in French Language. Mount Mary Training College is situated in the Eastern Region, Manya Krobo. It is a Roman Catholic school with a priest all the time. The college has a satellite dish which permits students to receive lessons directly from France. The school enjoys financial support from the French government from time to time.

After I submitted the registration form, we had to travel to the school to write an entrance exam. As the only French Training College in the country by then, every year, students from every part of Ghana often choose it. But because of limited classrooms and the pressure on other facilities, the school could not admit everyone. Based on this reason, there is always an entrance exam as a factor to cut down the number of students. It was like a competition. In 1994, about four hundred students applied to the school but only over one hundred students were going to be admitted.

I was also among the four hundred students who showed up for the entrance exams followed by an interview. The exam was conducted in the French Language. We did French dictation, grammar, comprehension in French, and oral text in French Laboratory. Just after the exams, an interview was conducted. The French Department teachers marked all the papers under thorough supervision by the Director of Projects from France. While teachers were busily marking the papers, students sat under the shady trees with dejected faces, waiting for their fate.

When you look at the number of students, you would be wondering in your mind if you were going to be admitted. Later in the afternoon, we were assembled for the grand results. The director of the Projects supervised the whole exams to ensure that only qualified students were chosen. On that day, luckily for me, my name was mentioned and by that I got admission to Mount Mary Training College. About one hundred and over students got admission on that day.

We could not report to school in the first term due to administrative procedures. On the 16th of January 1995, we officially arrived to Momaco (short form of Mount Mary Training College). It is a beautiful school with pretty classrooms. The classrooms have air conditioning. The satellite dish enables us to receive direct information from France. The school has a big library (bibliotheque), and the French Department is furnished with various equipments and electronic gadgets for our practical works. The atmosphere was strictly in French.

Students used to do their practical attachment in neighboring French-speaking countries like La Cote D'Ivoire (Ivory Coast), Togo, Benin etc. The French Department and Ghana Education Service had also sponsored some of them before to France for such practical exercises. At the time my group got there, the program was temporally stopped. I was not happy about it but that was the case for my group. We did not get the opportunity to travel to any French-speaking countries for practical training. But when my group finished the college, the outside program was brought back.

Teacher Training College in those days was characterized by tough disciplinary measures than what I witnessed even in Secondary School. What we go through in Secondary School was no where near in terms of discipline. The assumption was that you were going to be a classroom teacher and as such, you should be more discipline in the first place in order to discipline children in the classroom. As a teacher, you will be involved in absolute developmental stages of school children, hence the need for you to get yourself acquainted with character training.

We were therefore taught in training college the various roles of the classroom teacher. The impact you will make on children would be greatly appreciated in the long round as a teacher. Good values, Ghanaian customs, and character training are just a few expectations of teachers under training. At Mount Mary Training College, we had the principal's assembly and morning devotions under Catholic doctrines. You did not misbehave and expect to go scot-free. We had a college prefect and house leaders. We had visiting hours. The third-year students were the seniors of the college and were responsible for enforcing rules and regulations.

The training lasted for three years, and teachers received Teacher's Certificate "A" from the University of Cape Coast. Subjects offered by then were English Language, Education,

French Language, English Literature, Basic Mathematics, Basic Science, Agricultural Science, Cultural Studies, Physical Education, Ghanaian Languages (Ewe, Twi, etc.), Teaching Practice, and Long Essay Writing. During the first year, students will go through four weeks of Teaching Practice in Manya Krobo Primary and surrounding schools. You have to graduate in the third year with French, Education, Literature in the English Language and English Language itself. We finally, have to write a long essay under a supervision of a House Master with a chosen topic of your own or given to you. These long essays are either written in English Language or in French Language.

There were do or die exams in the second year called Part 1 and the final one in third year called Part 2. You have to pass these exams in order to advance to third year. If you fail these exams, you will repeat and do the make-up. We have to do another four weeks of Teaching Practice in second year as well. This time, it is done in Junior Secondary School. In the course of the four weeks of our teaching practice, you have to prepare a lesson plan with measurable and achievable objectives. This lesson plan would be submitted to your teacher on campus ahead of time for approval. Any deviation from the lesson plan was cancelled by your supervisor and you have to prepare another one.

When your supervisor approved your lesson note that was just one aspect of it; The next process was to search for a variety of concrete teaching materials in order to substantiate your lesson in the classroom. Student teachers were also reminded of the design of their teaching aids. The colors of your teaching materials were very important. If you are not able to find the actual teaching material, you have to improvise it as a sort of substitution.

Few days ahead of the lesson the student teacher has to go through his or her notes so as to master the various stages of the note. You will be informed of your college teacher coming through to supervise you or you will be caught unaware in most cases just to ensure we are doing the right thing.

The supervisors evaluated us on the application of subject knowledge and skills, motivational means for the students, quality assurance, and boldness. Evaluation lasted with ten to fifteen minutes after which you are called in one corner of the classroom for review. All your strong points are elevated with suggestions as to how to improve upon on your next visitation. You are evaluated on chronological presentation of lessons, self-confidence, relaxing during teaching, good posture in the classroom (ensuring that while teaching, you are not blocking your pupils' view), exhibiting eye contact, proper use of teaching materials, and how quickly you are able to turn your nervousness into positive nature. These are some of the things our college teachers look for during teaching practice.

As a student-teacher in training, we are faced with the daunting task of molding our pupils for a sustainable growth through meaningful education. Student in practice cannot avoid a classroom presentation of lessons. The fear of anxiety and thinking of embarrassing yourself in front of your students were some of the obstacles of teachers in those days on teaching practice.

The teacher training program requires heavy funding in order to sustain it. At the time I was in training, we used to enjoy the Ghana government's funding in the form of allowances in every month as a supplement for our education. We the students named it "Allawa." That was what helped some of us to finish Teacher Training course. We used to line up in front of the school's disbursing office for the money. One by one, the student teacher's name is mentioned, and you have to verify particulars, sign for it, and the amount of money due to you was paid. When the money is eventually in your hand, counted at that moment, you will hear students shouting "Allawa oooo."

What to do next? Of course, we spent the money during teaching practice buying teaching materials and making sure that we had everything needed for our lessons. We also fed ourselves by going to eat "Banku," (banku is a local food), and after teaching practice, some of us passed by "Brukutu" or "Pito" (local drinks) before returning to campus. I could remember in those days how some of my Annex house friends used to frequently go to the basement to buy Banku and eat. We were always on time (early birds). Those of us who were regular to buy the food to eat were called (regu). I was one of them. The rests were Ben Morti, Jean Nufe, Nicholas and one—Francis. We did not spare the food at all because we needed that to supplement dining hall food.

Every Sunday, we attended Roman Catholic Church service led by the priest. Church service always lasted for some hours. Some students put on (Kente) cloth and (Batakali). After church service, the various prayer groups gathered in their meeting places. The Spiritual Union (SU) mostly meets in the basement of the dining hall. The Moslem students too had a venue for their five times prayers. We had other social groups such as the French Club, The Association of the Ewe Group, The Akans, The Dangbes, and the Northern Groups. Each cultural association took turns to entertain the student body on entertainment day, which was usually held on Saturday night. We, the Ewe, are noted for (Borborbor) and (Agbadza). Come and see me dancing borborbor. I used to be quiet but during borborbor moment, it was no joke.

Just like it is said, "all work and no play make Jack a dull boy," student-teachers too, needed to take some time off from busy classroom tasks so that they will not be boring. The usual entertainment on Saturday night featured a disco dance. Come and witness student teachers on the dance floor! That was the occasion where secret student teacher lovers were revealed. They came out from their hideout to dance.

At Momaco, we used the talking drums as the medium of communication instead of the bell. It is part of Ghanaian rich cultural heritage. The talking drums were the ancient means of communicating information and they are still being used in Ghana. The drums are also used during traditional festivals, grand ceremonies, and rituals during burials of elders and traditional chiefs. These drums are the embodiment of Ghanaian cultural heritage and traditions. History has it that at the time the early colonial masters came to the coast of Africa, they realized that the indigenous Africans were spreading the news of their arrival through these talking drums.

Sporting activities were also organized in Mount Mary Training College for student teachers. We had inter-house competitions so that students who performed harder were selected to form the college team. The activities were in two categories: track and field events. There was an opening ceremony, which was performed by the principal or a representative from Manya Krobo District Education Service. Student-teachers were made aware of sporting events as an attractive discipline and as such, should behave well. The event was usually held during one or two weeks. Mount Mary has enough space for a nice size football field. Students mostly weeded it with cutlasses. The football field is covered with green grass as a result of the tropical weather and frequent rainfalls. The inter house competition provided us with a lot of excitement and a break away from intensive academic works.

Students prepare the football field and the track events with proper markings and goal posts. Sometimes, when a student teacher misbehaved toward a senior, he or she was given a portion of the football field to weed. You have to be well-mannered and well-behaved in order to avoid cutting up the grass as a punishment. We were required to bring a cutlass and broom to school. Students who performed well were rewarded with prizes as a form of motivation. Some set new records. Sometimes tension almost mounted during these occasions. We sang songs to cheer our houses. My house, Adzikpo used to have some outstanding runners. One particular guy by the name Francis can really run. He set records and broke other existing ones. He was mostly judged as the best athlete in 100 m and can run in the relay team as well.

The Independence Day parade brought another opportunity for us to go to the Somanya town. As boarders, we were always on campus. To get out of campus required written permission, which must be endorsed by your house master through your house captain. Your identity card would be signed, and your name written down until you come back to report yourself. I personally did not like those long and time-consuming formalities. So, occasions of this nature brought themselves and I love every bit of it. We have to do a lot of marching preparations in ahead of time.

On Independence Day itself, student-teachers were divided into two groups and sent to the various parade grounds. It is worthy to note that Ghana is the first Sub-Saharan African nation to gain Independence from British colonial rule on the sixth of March 1957. Since then, the Independence Day is organized each year to honor those who fought and shed their blood for the independence struggle. We the student teachers at Mount Mary Training College were also part of that colorful marching ceremony in Manya Yilo Krobo in Eastern Region of Ghana.

History has it that it was on the sixth of March 1957 that the first President of Ghana, Dr. Kwame Nkrumah proclaimed the Independence of Ghana from British rule. Nkrumah told Ghanaians that "At long last, the battles have ended and Ghana, your beloved country, is free forever." Dr. Kwame Nkrumah further stated that "The independence of Ghana is meaningless unless it is linked up to the total liberation of Africa." At the Eastern Regional level or District level, a government representative in the person of District Chief Executive will stand in order to acknowledge all participants marching in honor of the parade.

We the student-teachers were there as well. Other agencies included are the Fire Service, the Ghana Police Service, Primary School Pupils, Junior Secondary School, Voluntary Organizations, and Senior Secondary School Students just to mention a few. A government representative will deliver the keynote address, after which awards are given to deserving people. Traditional Chiefs often ride high in their palanquins to the parade ground. In the nutshell, that was how I could remember Independence celebration by then in Somanya town as a student teacher and we were right back to campus.

Back at Mount Mary Training College, we used to observe Roman Catholic Retreat Week. It was a week of intensive meditation, devotion and observance of quiet moments. That particular week was dedicated to unusual lives of holiness and devotion to God. The Roman Catholic Priest of the school led student teachers through a special guided prayer section of spiritualism. During the retreat week, no one left the school campus. Most of the time was spent in the dining hall for prayers, reading of the Bible, and reflecting over our lives.

A guest priest was equally invited to join the student body. The atmosphere on campus appeared as if we were in a cemetery. We pondered over our lifestyles. Nobody made a noise or could even shout. We learnt a great deal of Christian values that could draw us to love one another. The prayer sections helped us to love one another. It also helped us to break down all the obstacles of depression, isolation, and loneliness. It was really a touching moment to contemplate and ponder over your life. I felt it provided holy nourishment for our soul.

The final year of Teacher Training College was a busy one. We had to do the last intensive teaching practice for one month and also write an external examination from the University of Cape Coast. When we left, student teachers were doing one full year teaching practice in the field before returning to campus. Exams time in school was nerve wracking and very important. Once the last paper is written, you are done. You are out of Teacher Training College, awaiting results. In June 1997, we took the final papers and that was it. Before you leave school campus, you have to choose your three regions you would like to go and teach. These three stations were for the sake of paperwork. It means that you can be posted to wherever your services are needed.

If you don't get your first choice, you can try your second choice and third one. At the same time, when you choose to go to a particular region, your name may end up in a different region which you have not in the first place chosen, nor dreamt of. That was exactly the situation in which I found myself in. My friend Confidence too attended Peki Training College and later was posted to teach in Kpando town.

MY THREE YEARS
TEACHING SERVICE

I completed Mount Mary Training College in June 1997, and left campus to my brother, Dr. Ankuvie Augustine in Donkorkroam. He was the District Director of Health Services in Afram Plains by then. The Presbyterian Hospital was under his care in those days. The hospital is the major one located in the Afram plains District. The district is believed to be deprived from other ones in Ghana and it is surrounded by lakes.

Accessibility to the place is through ferries and boats. Big cargo trucks are mostly internal means of transportation. The area is noted for Agricultural products. The activities of the people of Donkorkrom are mainly farming, hunting, and fishing. Dr. Ankuvie was farming at the time I went there. As a son of a cocoa farmer, even though he became a medical doctor, he was still interested in farming activities. I stayed with him until the teacher training posting came out. While I was waiting for my results, I accompanied several laborers to do clearing and preparation of farming lands with cutlasses. It is a very daunting and arduous task since it is done manually.

My brother used to farm on a large scale, stored the harvest and in turn sold it. Some of the farmers in the Donkorkroam area practiced what is referred to as co-operative farming. It is the system where the farmers in the same community took turns to assist each other in the course of weeding and harvesting farm products. Some of the farmers did backyard farming while others were engaged in livestock rearing. Most farmers in this area did not want to allow their children to even attend school in those days because of their intensive farming activities.

Whenever the harvest of Dr. Ankuvie's maize farm was done, a large crowd of village folks were mobilized to carry the products from the distant farms to where there was access to tipper trucks which would then carry the harvested maize to his storage. I was also overseeing all these activities for him at a time when he returned from our village Wusuta, with bad news for me. He informed me upon arrival that the Teacher Training posting for that physical year was out and unfortunately for me, I was posted to the Northern part of Ghana.

In actual fact, I received the message with mixed feelings because all my three choices were denied. I initially chose Volta Region, Eastern Region, and Central Region but when the posting came out, my name appeared on Upper West, the capital of which is Wa. The most annoying aspect of it was that my name was the first one on the Wa list of newly posted teachers. I believed we were nine teachers from Mount Mary College posted to Wa in September 1997. One more time, I became angry. It was some kind of "Man proposes, but God disposes" for me. Little did I know that Almighty God had something in store for me in this far place which will positively change my life.

My wishes were not being satisfied. Little did I know that God put a treasure down for me in the North of Ghana to go and find. I will let you know later. In one month prior to reporting to my duty station at Wa, my brother Augustine, gave me some money to get prepared for the journey. I left Donkorkrom and went back to our village Wusuta. I spent few days relaxing and off again to Ho, the Volta Regional capital. My plan was to visit a friend's uncle, who had earlier on promised to assist me in getting a station in the Volta Region to teach. I met him as planned but he said there was nothing he could do to assist me any longer.

According to him, the Teacher Training posting used to be a regional issue, but things got changed. He stated he wished he could have assisted me but that particular year, the posting was done nationally. At that moment, I realized that there was nothing I could do other than get ready to depart to the North to teach. I left Ho to Hohoe where my sister Mawuse was staying. I intended to buy the items I needed over there so that I can set off to go to Wa.

One Sunday afternoon, while I was packing my belongings into my bag, I overheard my sister talking to someone under the shady tree in our compound at Hohoe. This man comes from Wusuta. He happened to come by to pay us a visit. I guessed while they were having a conversation, my sister raised the issue about me going to the far North to teach without even knowing anybody there. My sister was worried about me leaving the house for the first time to stay on my own without any family member around to guide me. This man asked my sister to call me.

When I came out, he requested for a pen and a paper so that he can refer me to his friend who was working at Social Security Bank (SSB) by then at Wa. He assured me that he was going to call his friend on the telephone ahead of time before I got there. I was little bit relieved that somebody was going to welcome me when I arrive. Lo and behold, I left Hohoe to go to Tema, where my brother Paul was staying.

I spent the weekend with him. Early on Monday morning, he accompanied me to State Transport Corporation's station, where I would board the Bus to Wa.

We finally got to the bus station. Paul and I sat down, and after a while he had to leave. He entered into a taxi and waved to me. In fact, when Paul left, I felt lonely and started shedding tears. The fear of an unknown place was crossing my mind every now and then. I could not help but cry. Have you ever been in a situation where a family member escorts you to board a vehicle? I believe you can imagine it for yourself.

Basically, I broke down emotionally. On my way back to the station when my brother left, I spotted a college friend also walking with his mother to the same station. I approached him immediately and asked him whether he was going to Wa as well. He nodded his head in agreement. I became happy and pulled myself together. There came a time where my luggage was charged and paid for. Luggage is charged based on the weight. Most of the time in Ghana, when boarding a commercial vehicle, buses, trotro, etc, the driver's mate or the conductor would charge all your belongings.

Lo and behold, the STC bus left Accra heading toward the north. Departures were strictly on a schedule. You needed to purchase a ticket in advance. The bus often waits in a row to depart when it is fully loaded. The buses are provided with maintenance facilities in some cities for any possible breakdown. The journey from Accra to Wa was very rocky and adventurous. If I am correct, it takes fifteen to eighteen hours from Accra to reach Wa. When the bus leaves Accra today, it will reach Wa early morning tomorrow. The bus traveling to the north is always loaded to capacity. If you miss the bus, there is trouble for you. We had traffic issues from Accra to Kumasi, the second largest city of Ghana. I realized that part of the road was paved while the other part was dusty. Such were the conditions of the road in those days.

Drivers have to drive on such unsafe roads every day. This reminds me of the poor infrastructure system in my country by then. We had some stop-over for food, rest, and attended restrooms. The popular stops are Kumasi, Techiman, Bamboe, and Bole. Despite the bad nature of the road, the bus runs very fast. There are always two drivers in one bus. One drives up to a place, and another one takes turn until it arrives in Wa. In Ghana, STC (State Transport Company) buses are just like the Greyhound ones in America.

The bus finally arrived in Wa early morning the following day. We got out and picked up our bags and suitcases. The two of us walked to the Wa district educational office with the help of one good Samaritan. The office was still closed because it was early morning. We sat down on a bench in front of the office waiting for the workers to show up. By seven thirty to eight a.m, the workers started showing up. The first arrival asked us who we were and the nature of our business at that early morning.

My friend and I told him that we were newly posted French teachers from the Southern Ghana to the Upper West Region. We were brought into the district office with our dirty luggage. We found out that nine of us were posted to the region and three French teachers would be sub-posted to the various districts of Wa. Luckily for me, my name being the first on the list earned me a place in Wa town. Unfortunately for my friend, he had to travel again for two days in order to get to his station, Tumu.

He became angry and unhappy. The two of us thought we were going to be in town, but it did not happen. That was how we got separated. I asked one of the office personnel to take me to my school. I sat on motor bike with this man and off I was taken to my school, Fallahia Junior Secondary School. It is Moslem established school. I was dropped under one mango tree where all the teachers were sitting. The man who brought me to the school spoke Wale, the dialect spoken in the area. I believed he was introducing me to them as the new French Teacher of the school.

All of sudden, I started hearing the term Monsieur, the French word for Mr. One teacher escorted me to the head teacher's office and introduced me to him. After that, I had a few conversations with him. I filled out some papers and equally signed my name to indicate that I have reported to my duty station. He asked whether I knew anybody in Wa town because of accommodation issues. It was this time that I mentioned the name of Mr. Wisdom Sagoe of SSB Bank. I told my head teacher that I have been referred to Mr. Wisdom and he was aware of my coming. My head teacher took me to Social Security Bank (SSB) so that we could locate him. We got to the bank to realize that he left to Accra for a refresher course.

One bank worker took me to his wife (Sister Pat) in her shop. It was then that I realized we even knew each other but I did not know that she was married to Mr. Sagoe. Sister Pat welcome me to Wa town. She later informed me that her husband left a message behind concerning my arrival. Getting to evening time, we left for home at Kpaguri (the residential area of Wa). After two weeks, Mr. Sagoe returned from his trip (Accra).

My life had therefore begun in Wa in Upper West Regional capital of Ghana. For the sake of those people who don't know, Ghana was divided into ten regions by then and Wa is one of them. From our house at Kpaguri to the town was about three to four miles. Bicycles are the most frequent means of transportation. You better learn how to ride them, otherwise you will suffer. Mr. Sagoe has a sizable family. The names of the kids are Effe, Mabina, Sami, Delali, and Sister Pat.

As I indicated earlier on, the capital of Upper West Region is Wa. Majority of the people are moslems. The language spoken here is Wala. The paramount chief of the Wala people is called Wa-Na. They have another tribe by the name of Dagaare. Their popular food is called T-zed. The inhabitants are mainly farmers and traders. The crops grown usually are groundnuts, yams, corn, millets. Brukutu and pito are some local drinks in the area. Some of the places in town are Upland Hotel, Tiegbe.

I had to walk from Kpaguri to Fallahia JSS. Even though it is within Wa town, it is quite a distance. Just after one week, Mr. Wisdom Sagoe bought me a bicycle to use. From that time until I left Wa, it became my immediate means of transportation. Throughout the three northern regions, the use of bicycles and motorcycles are very rampant. Anyone coming to these areas needs to learn how to operate them.

As the only French teacher at the school, I had to prepare a lesson plan to teach JSS 1, 2 and 3. Each class contained about 30 to thirty-five students with A and B. By the time I finished teaching from F1, F2, and F3, then I became tired. One of the Form 3 classes was also given to me to mentor. Every morning, I had to call the register. Some of the students were regular to class while others did not see the need for education. They preferred rearing cattle than coming to school. You would be surprised to see students in school with no pen nor book to write with. Terminal exams was often a busy moment for me since I had to sit down to mark several papers.

Mr. Wisdom and I were always hanging out in town. He worked in the SSB and came home mostly late in the night. But any slight chance he got we went out to have some drinks. Whenever he was off during the weekend, we went out to buy some guinea fowls and merrymaking started. His wife popularly known as Sister Pat would prepare either palm nut or groundnut soup with the guinea fowls for us. Banku would be cooked. By the time the food was ready, we would have gone out with the motor bike to buy Akpeteshie or Kasapreku. He usually invited a few friends to come over too. Before we began to eat, everyone took a few shots of the alcohol. It is our custom. Together, we sit round the table and enjoy the meals.

It is part of the Ghanaian custom to have some drinks as appetizer before we sit down to eat fufu, banku, akple, kokonte (face the wall), tozafi, or sao-T-zed for short. These foods are eaten with the hand. They are not eaten with a spoon. It does not mean that the people of Africa eat such foods with hands because they don't have spoons in Africa. Just like Americans have thousands of spoons yet they use the hands to eat hamburgers the same way we also use the hands to eat our traditional dishes. Someone wanted to know why Africans eat fufu with their hands. Is it because they don't have spoons in Africa? This is just one of the questions I get at work in US Navy.

Other two French teachers who were stationed in Wa town with me were Mr. Selasi Adzimah and Mr. Nestor Henyo. The three of us all taught in Wa schools. The rests were distributed among other districts within the region. They equally came to Mr. Sagoe's house where I was staying. As usual, we either prepare light soup with guinea fowl or goat meat. With some shots of Akpeteshie, come and see us sweating.

On another occasion, we gathered together to drink "pito." It is the local drink brewed in Wa and the rest of the northern regions. It is an alcoholic drink which is made out of millet. It is sweet wild in terms of taste. Calabash is used to serve it. It is mainly done by women. The color of pito is golden yellow to dark brown. It has about three percent of alcohol and is very acidic. The other alcohol beverage drink is called burukutu. It is prepared from sorghum grains and served in the brewer's compound. They are income-generating activities of the women in the north of Ghana.

We the French teachers usually gathered at Wa Secondary School for a quarterly refresher course. During this time, all the French teachers all over the Wa Region were obligated to travel to this school. This refresher course lasted for one week. It was the French government's sponsorship training which was meant to equip all JSS teachers of French Language on the teaching field. At the end of the course, the program coordinator reimbursed us for transportation, food and accommodation. While I was teaching at Fallahia JSS, my friend Selasi was teaching at another JSS in Wa town. Upper West Region being one of the deprived among other regions in Ghana by then, made it difficult for trained teachers to accept posting orders at that time. As such, some teachers reported and then left to the south.

Wa is characterized by a very high cost of motorized transportation system. A slight mistake can lead you to an accident. There are different seasons ranging from an intensive raining season to the worst dry season. The raining season starts in July up to September while the dust and cold season is between November and February. Dry season is known as the harmattan season. From February to April, you will experience very hot air. During that time, you have to open your window in order to sleep.

Wa district is most of the time dry. Even though the Upper West Region has a Savannah landscape, cattle are reared in the areas. Some of the agricultural products are yam, groundnuts, corn, millet, sorghum, and shea butter. Baobab and Dawadawa are very important trees for herbal medicines. The seed of the Dawadawa tree is used to make soup (Dawadawa soup).

My brother Sagoe's good customer relationship at SSB in those days earned him a lot of friends. One of his outstanding female friends is called Vincentia Votere. She worked at the National Bureau of Small-Scale Industry (NBSSI). Mr. Sagoe introduced me to her as a new brother in town and he needed her to be showing me around anytime she was free. A few days later the initial introduction, she rode her loud motorbike to pick me from the house to hanging out until Mr. Sagoe was off from Banking works.

Vincentia's mother used to brew pito and sell it in their house. Anytime I was picked up to their house, we drank her mother's pito. Sometimes, I, Mr. Sagoe, and Vincentia together with SSB driver, we emptied several small pots of pito. Vincentia's family always welcome us. They are very hospitable and cheerful people. Vincentia's sister by the name of Bernadette would quickly prepare T-zed with dawadawa soup for us while we were drinking pito and cracking jokes.

Most of the time, by two o'clock in the afternoon when I closed from school, I would pass by her office. We usually sat down and chat and after that I would be on my way back to home. Whenever she was off too, she would ride her motorbike to my house in order to pick me up to her house. Whenever we were out, guess where we were? Pito base of course!! As I said earlier on, in almost every household, pito is being sold. At some bases, they prepared a fresh pork soup and sold it alongside with the alcoholic drink.

One day after school, I made a stop over at her office. We were having a conversation and she cut me short by talking about US Visa Lottery Form. According to her, someone gave her the application form and wanted her to make some copies for her. She wanted me to know if I was aware of it. In actual fact, I had never heard of it before that you can be in

Ghana and can win a visa lottery and be given a visa to travel to the U.S. I did not know anything about that.

What happened next was that she handed me a copy of the U.S. Visa Lottery Form to go and fill and post it. According to her, maybe I might be lucky to win it and travel to the U.S. one day. When she gave me the paper, I put it back on the table and told her that I was not interested in it. Moreover, I was not sure of winning it. Basically, I did not believe that when I fill a mere form in Ghana and post it to the U.S, and after some months I will receive a letter telling me that I won it. I could not believe it.

My friend Vincentia re-echoed her previous statement to me that I may not believe it, but she still wants me to take the form home and try my luck on it. I finally took it anyway and put it inside a folder and took it home. I did not even try to fill it or read through it. I kept it there and forgot about posting it on time.

Two weeks later, she visited me to find out whether I filled out the Visa Lottery paperwork. I told her that I did not even know the whereabout of the form. I looked through my books and later found it in the folder in which I earlier put it in. Together, we filled it out and went to post office to post it. Surprisingly, in three months, I received a big envelope from USA.

Dear reader of this book, I want to inform you that the letter I received from the United States of America is what has brought me to here today. I came back from school and met a letter. You will agree with me that whenever you get a letter, a simple look at the envelope can reveal to you where it comes from. That was exactly what I did and realized that it came from the U.S. I was wondering who knew me from America. I forgot of the Visa Lottery issue.

I opened the envelope and started reading it. There, I quickly remembered of the Visa Lottery Form given to me to fill. The letter initially congratulated me for winning the U.S. Visa Lottery. My mind went back to the scenario of how everything happened. I jumped on my bicycle and off I went to my friend Vincentia at her office. I knocked, entered and gave it to her to read. She wanted to have an idea about it but I did not let her know of it until she read it and got the good news herself.

From the office, we went out to celebrate the news at the pito base. I was quite shocked about it because I doubted it, but it became a reality for the rest of my life. Such is the world!! I am in America today as a result of that lady called Vincentia comment about the American Visa Lottery. Her remarkable inspiration led me to reach this stage. A real turning point in my life. This brings into my mind about opportunity. It came my way and I grabbed it. I needed it, but did not plan for it.

I kept corresponding until I received another letter asking me to attend an interview at the American Embassy in Accra. The day of the interview came, and I was there. They went through all my particulars and realized that I was missing an affidavit of support. At this point, the consular representative advised me to look for someone who lived in the United States in order to provide me with an affidavit of support. My brother, Dr. Ankuvie consulted one of his friends in Chicago on this issue with Mr. Komla Penty.

In a few months later, Stephanie, the wife of Komla sent me an affidavit of support. Upon receiving it, I went back to the U.S. Embassy in Accra. The affidavit was reviewed thoroughly and at the end of the day, the Visa was issued to me to travel to America. What a miracle!!! I have not been planning in my life to travel to the U.S. but a mere push from Lady Vincentia, introduced to me by my host, Mr. Wisdom, I am now pursuing my American dream. I believe that you can see so far how God used Mr. Wisdom Sagoe to introduce me to Vincentia and her in turn, gave me the U.S. Visa Lottery idea. An idea I did not have myself, yet it was the one which has made a significant impact in my life. Did you also remember that I did not want to travel to the Northern part of Ghana to teach? The place I was going to and was crying about, I ended up getting my luck over there.

This is how wonderful the world is. Isn't it? Are you following my story up to this stage? I hope you do. If really you are following the story, you can see how one thing led to another. I wanted to go to Sixth Form, but I failed one subject (English Language), and had to go to Likpe Secondary School to re-write it. Just after that, I changed my mind from going to Sixth Form to Teacher Training College.

I finished Teacher Training College and wanted to stay in the Volta Region to teach yet I was posted to Wa in the Upper Region. It was against my will to go to Wa, the far North to teach French Language. In the course of staying in Wa, my host—Mr. Wisdom Sagoe felt that I was new to Wa town, so I needed friends to take me out in order to get myself acquainted to that new environment. Doing so, I met an opportunity. I doubted it but God proved me wrong. I hope you dear readers of this book are following my story!!

Do you remember how there are things in your mind that you would like to get done in an orderly manner? What I am trying to say is that you may sometimes expect life the usual way or straightforward. But based on my own experience, you would not understand why certain things happened just to obstruct your scale of preferences. Your wishes and expectations may be deterred at a point in time. You would even wish to commit suicide. While all these things are happening to you, your close family members who are alive may ignore you or pretend. If you ask them for financial help, they will find every reason not to assist you.

Some will deliberately seek for your downfall. But I just want to say that don't lose hope or give up.

I am letting you know that do not be afraid or scared when you come across impediments on your usual way of life. Any unexpected happening in your life is a test down the road of greater life to come in the future. Any event that seems to be shutting down your present dreams could be rather redirecting your path to achieving your ultimate goals in life eventually. I will prefer a tragedy in early life and a comedy toward the end of a story. Such occurrences (despair, frustrations, misery, loss of hope, fear, illness, injury, betrayal, marriage, and divorce etc.) are roadblocks that you have to deal with whether you like it or not.

While i was in a desperate situation, an opportunity emerged from nowhere. I badly needed it but did not know how it was going to come by. Sitting down contemplating too, is not the solution. You have to get out there and start doing something meaningful about your situation. I had to travel from the South to the North of Ghana in order to meet the opportunity of coming to the United States of America. Isn't that interesting to hear?

You always have to be prepared for any eventuality in life. I never thought of traveling to the United States of America. But here I am!!! The boy born and raised in the middle of forest with endless darkness, with no electricity, or potable water, let alone telephone is now living in America. We used kerosine lamp to see and to study by then in the village (Akposso Bibi), in Togo.

Growing up I have been hearing the popular saying that "Wounders never end," and that is the world we live in. You maybe doubting all that is happening to you. I can assure you that as long as you keep trying your best and trusting your God, you will one day be victorious. It is not easy when your parents have so many mouths to feed and bills to pay. In our case, we had plenty of our farm food to eat but meeting our educational needs was not easy a joke because we were plenty. My father had 12 kids and 3 were grown then 9 others came to follow.

Out of the 9, one female died in 1999. That was my immediate sister by the name Edith Yawavi Ankuvie. Earlier on, the second born of my father in the person of Patrick Kofi Ankuvie traveled to Spain in 1990. In 1993, we received a letter with some pictures that he died and was even buried there. Patrick's mother-popularly known as Kumanor was based at Kute, a border town between Ghana and Togo. The rests of us toiled hard in the village in the middle of cocoa farm. The hardships of life will be forcing you to plan certain things in your mind that nobody knows about. You can imagine the anxieties if your plans cannot be achieved the way you want them to fall in place. This is where hope is very important. Envisioning a better future for oneself is a motivating factor.

MY JOURNEY TO
THE UNITED STATES
OF AMERICA

Right after I got a Visa to travel, I went back to Wa in Upper West Region of Ghana. I went to school as usual to teach. As I went about doing my day-to-day job, another conflict started generating in my mind. I looked confident outside, yet there was fight going on inside me. It was about how to raise money to get prepared for my journey to the United States of America. In the middle of all your troubles, an opportunity emerges from nowhere, yet you did not personally have financial resources to support it. Was I going to let it go or capitalize on it to make a difference not only in your own life but in the life of others?

Mr. Wisdom Sagoe and Vincentia Votere through whom I got the opportunity from, informed me that they wished they could equally assist me financially to travel to the U.S. I am making a point here—that is how you can get a clear chance, but lack of money can make it impossible for you to utilize it. This happens all the time. Someone's clear chance can slip away as a result of financial sponsorship. Dr. Ankuvie Augustine, my brother made it happened for me. Even though I did not have the money to support the opportunity, he assisted me. May God continue to bless him in abundance.

I basically taught French Language at Fallahia JSS from 1997 up to 2000. So I left Wa around April 2000 to my favorite abode, Doctor's place by then—Donkorkroam in the Afram plains. At the time of departing from Wa, I couldn't tell my headteacher that I got a visa, so I was traveling to the United States. I wrote a permission letter that I was attending a family funeral and I moved out of Wa. I was not happy that I was leaving my students. However, I wanted to search for a greener pasture.

Little did I know much about the United States of America. But I had an idea of few American dollars and their equivalency in Ghanaian cedi. A few friends and close relatives who heard that I was traveling to the States all expressed their desires to assist me with money for preparations. When the moment came for final preparations, ask me how many of those people actually came forward to help me with money? None of them except Doctor Ankuvie.

Anyone who promised to help financially came back with excuses. I was not surprised because my brother already told me that they were not going to fulfill their promises. He said that I should wait and see!! And it was just as he predicted. This also reminded me of African mentality toward anyone who is about to travel to the United States of America. All that they want to do is to get rid of your opportunity of coming to the U.S. or Europe. What do you think is the reason? Perhaps, when you get to the States, you would get a good job with good pay which will be far better than them.

Someone can even use "African Voodo or juju" to kill or prevent you from achieving your dream/aim. You can even go mad or fall sick and die unexpectedly. Some people can put uncurable sickness on you and you will suffer slowly till you die painfully. I am being serious!!! We are crying for progress and development in Africa, yet we are the same people who are not ready for changes. We are still obstacles in our ways and looking for manna to fall from heaven for us. We are also looking anxiously for foreign assistance but ready to send our own human brains to the grave by any means necessary.

Behaviors of this nature force some Africans to stay for good in the U.S. and Europe. Someone might be thinking that I am washing our own African dirty laundry in public, yet I am speaking about the truth. If you need to call a spade a spade, feel free to do so. I hate beating around the bush. Well, this is another topic I need to tell you later into details.

I did the final preparations at our home Wusuta, in the Volta Region. Early morning on the fourth of July 2000, Dr. Augustine Ankuvie, Mawuse Ankuvie, and Moses Ankuvie, all saw me off at Kotoka International Airport in Accra. We arrived in Accra around ten a.m. and went to check on flight schedules. I was supposed to board the airline by the name Wabash. It is an American airline that came to Ghana for the first time. The plane was initially scheduled for afternoon flight. But we got to the airport to realize that it was leaving at noon rather.

Dr. Ankuvie and one of his friends went out to change cedi into dollars for me. By the time they came back, it was time for me to go. So, they could not go and change more money for me. I had to take those few dollars and off I went. I had earlier on checked my luggage in already. I quickly hurried up to the departure hall. After going through all necessary security procedures, I walked into Wabash Airline. That was the first time this particular airline came to Ghana.

In no time before I realized it, we were in the air already. In fact, that was my first time of boarding a plane. I felt dizzy when the plane was taking off the ground. I left Ghana on the fourth of July 2000. The plane had a stopover for fuel in Portugal. It was at the airport, and nobody was allowed to get out of the plane. Some passengers stood at the entrance in order to see the area view but could not get out.

Early in the morning on the fifth of July 2000, the plane touched down and we arrived in New York city, the United States of America. After going through an intensive immigration search, I handed my package from the American Embassy in Accra (Ghana) to them. They looked through my documents and stamped inside my Passport and gave it back to me. I asked whether that was all, and the custom official said yes. I proceeded to the luggage claim area. Within some minutes, I got my bag.

Even though I got to New York, that was not the end of my destination. I had to continue my journey to Chicago. When I found out how much it will cost me to get to Chicago by air, I realized that the pocket money I had on me was not enough to make it. So, a good Samaritan came out with the idea of taking the Greyhound bus from New York to Chicago. Finally, this idea worked out. That first day, how to get to the Greyhound station in New York became a little bit of a problem.

But I finally found it and was able to purchase a ticket. At dawn, on the fifth of July, the Greyhound bus left New York in route to Chicago. We had several stopovers on the way and arrived in the evening. I was really tired. Luckily, Dr. Ankuvie's friend Mr. Komla Penty was at the station to welcome me. He took me to Du Paul University Campus in Chicago. By then, he was doing a course over there.

The following day, I filled out paperwork for a Social Security number. Instantly, I was given a temporary number which I could use to start looking for a job. The Social Security Identification card was supposed to come in two weeks' time. At that time, my host in the person of Komla, discussed an idea with me as a shortcut to get a job. Realizing that I was running out of pocket money, I agreed to his proposal.

He wanted me to join him and the rest of their Buddhist congregation to chant. According to him, at the end of the day he will introduce me to their leadership, and they would assist me in getting a job in no time. As a new person in town, I had to stay indoors until he was free to come and take me around. In the afternoon, we went to chant. So a few days after I got to Chicago, I began to practice Buddhism. It was not easy for me during the first two days. Imagine sitting at one place and chanting for hours!!

I observed how everyone was chanting, and I imitated them. I realized that they pressed their palms together at chest level while chanting. I noticed they had a bell around and at a point in time, it was rung while chanting. I was made to understand that chanting in Buddhism is a form of meditation or a veneration to purify the mind of an individual. Also, I got to know that in Buddhism, there are "Four Noble Truths," which are birth, aging, sickness, and death. Everything, therefore, revolves around these four noble truths.

As the tradition goes, if you are a new member during such gathering, you have to be introduced at the end of the chanting. So, once we finished the chanting, my host did the introduction, and I was welcome awesomely. He then told the gathering that I was looking for a job so if anyone could assist me in any way, he would appreciate it. In a couple of days, one tall and light skin lady just came out and asked me whether I was interested in working in a hotel.

I quickly answered yes, and she took me to the Ritz-Carlton Chicago, A Four Seasons Hotel to apply for a job. She basically referred me and as such, I was hired in no time. I left Ghana in West Africa on the fourth of July 2000 and got here on the fifth. On the 17th of July 2000, I was hired at this hotel in downtown Chicago as an overnight housekeeper. Remember, I was staying in one of the students' rooms and we had to vacate this room within one month. I came at the time when university students were on vacation. I was lucky my host was doing a course in the school by then and was given a room in Corcoran Hall of DePaul University. He is married to a beautiful lady by the name of Stephanie, and they were staying at 556 W Aldine Ave by then. In the night, he would go to his wife, while I had the room to myself.

Even though I got the job, I was worried of where to sleep after one month's time given to us to vacate the hostel. Two weeks to vacating the room, my host kept on making some important telephone calls to some of his friends. I could remember how he spoke to some of his friends on the phone concerning me. He wanted to find out if they could temporarily accommodate me until I raised enough money to be on my own.

Some of the calls fell on deaf ears until one brother responded. He was my savior. This person accepted to take me home if only I could adjust myself to sleep in a little storage unit of their two bedrooms basement apartment. This brother and my savior is called Elikplim. He is from Ghana as well. He had one roommate called Jimmy, a white guy. The place I had to sleep was extra cold to the extent that I do not even know which word to describe it. I had no choice than to take it.

As soon as the land lady got to know that I was staying there, she increased the rent for my brother. I paid for that little storage unit that was turned into a sleeping place for me. I was there up to October 25th, 2000. Considering my situation, the timing and the far place I had come to, I accepted it in good faith. As one of overnight keepers in Ritz-Carlton Hotel, we cleaned restrooms, passageways, and vacuumed. Have you ever been in a situation where you don't like it, yet you cannot do anything about it?

All those conditions that I went through in Chicago, even though I did not like them, they made me stronger. Everyone appeared to be preoccupied as the pattern of life in America. You can be desperate in the U.S. and need help from left and right but not until that person is free with his or her work schedule, he or she cannot attend to you.

What I want people to know is that as you are growing, you need to identify that life may not be getting any easier for you as compared to when you were young. Your ability to withstand any condition that may come your way will be a determining factor in your next level of life. You may be hungry and don't have money to buy your next meal, but don't give up. You always have to start from somewhere and build up to your present stage.

I came here with one big traveling bag and a pair of shoes. I was ashamed of it but there was nothing I could do about it. I felt bad but could not do anything about it until I managed to get that job through chanting. I went to work with little food and came back to sleep with a few doughnuts in my stomach. Sometimes, I could not close my eyes to sleep in the night. Moreover, the storage unit was deplorable for a person to sleep in. But that was the reality on the ground, and I managed to endure it. Are you feeling me?

Today as I am writing this book, I am proud to let you know that those moments all reminded me of the past, and I worked hard to buy a condominium. The townhouse I bought had two bedrooms with one and a half baths, covered parking, a wood-burning fireplace, and a master bedroom with a walk-in closet. I equally put in effort to get a Degree in Bachelor of Science in Business Administration from Colorado Technical University with a concentration in Business Management.

I did not let all my sufferings affect me. I rather endured it and it became an experience for me. Elderly people back at home used to say, "experience is the best teacher." When I was young, I did not understand it but as at now, I have come to understand it. You need to make hay while the sun shines. I could have been living a good life but ever since I settled in America, I have been helping my family and all the people who assisted me to get to the top of the tree.

As a child who was born and raised in a village in Togo, my flashback is real. I gave a lot of credit to my parents and guardians. I spoke of the old saying that goes "experience is the best teacher." I don't know how you may interpret it, but to me, knowledge is acquired through so many ways. Some people go to school to acquire it, while others also learn it by doing it constantly on the job. Whatever you learn in school we all know it to be academic, while experience is gained through observation and doing it over and over again. Your house knowledge is very critical in your daily life. I can assure you that when you combine knowledge acquired in school with what your parents and guardians have taught you and your age, there is no way that you cannot overcome the hardship of life. In so doing, you will become an experienced person.

Now let us understand what it means by "Make hay while the sun shines." You do not just begin to act anyhow in life. Your situation or the situation you find yourself in should allow you to act wisely. Acting in time where someone have to help you to stand on your feet can jeopardize your chances in life. Maintain your composure and take control when your circumstance or condition even if it does not favor you or otherwise. You cannot make hay when the rain is falling frequently. You need the sun to dry your grass in order to make your hay. You may have to study the rainfall pattern before you cut the grass, if not, you cannot dry it.

While I was living in uptown Chicago, I had to catch the train each time to downtown Chicago for work. The cold weather did not favor me at all. It usually freezes in Chicago, and I could not stand it. I knew of the four Seasons (winter, summer, spring, and autumn) in terms of weather but did not know how intensive they were until I got here. When I was about to sleep, come and see the way I dressed up before I went to bed. Even after dressing up, I still have to use a thick cloth I brought here from Ghana as cover cloth.

When I boarded the train on my way back home, I sometimes doze and forget to get off when I arrived to the end of my destination. Before I realized, the train will by-pass my destination. There was nothing I could do than to sit down for the train to go round its routes until arriving before I could get down. My new host Elikplim and I used to share our views on life in general. I remembered how we used to go to African Market to buy food items each time we were paid.

I was shocked to see almost all the food stuffs we eat back at home in Ghana. The first time we visited and I saw them, I was really happy and felt at home even though I was far away from actual home. One day, he spoke to me about how he wanted to join the U.S Navy but could not due to some circumstances beyond his control. He suggested to me to join the Navy so that I can be financially sound. I thought about it the whole night and became interested in the educational aspect where the Navy will pay for your college through tuition assistance and GI Bill. I thought of it again in few nights and one day, I asked him to accompany me to the Navy Recruiting Station. And that was how I joined the Navy.

MY PARENTS AND GUARDIANS

My father was the breadwinner of the house. He was the third born of his father's children but became the head of the entire family when the first and second born all died. He then became the oldest son of his father. His father denied him of the opportunity to attend school as the tradition by then. Rather, his father asked him to assist on the farm so that he can cater for the younger ones. Out of the children his father gave birth to, three of them in addition to one woman survived: Nani, Ekpe (Stone), Kumah (who later died), and the only female-Bedu popularly known as Tasi Bedu (Aunty Bedu).

My brothers, sisters and I grew up to know three uncles and one aunty. As the tradition of the time, everyone traveled to buy forest land and cultivate that land into a cocoa farm as an income generating activity. My grandfather traveled to Akposso Bibi in Togo to acquire a piece of land. My father followed his father to Akposso and assisted his father to cultivate the land into cocoa plantation. The forest land was later given to our father as a gift for accepting his father's decision not to go to school but rather helped him on the land in order to raise money to cater for the subsequent ones.

My uncles and the only aunt were all sent to school but unfortunately, they all could not make it. They eventually dropped out of school. My father, Edward Mensah Ankuvie cultivated the forest land bought for him into a cocoa farm in Akposso Bibi in Togo. That was the place the nine of us who were under the care of my stepmother were brought up. This cocoa farm has generated a lot of family dispute between him, his brothers and only sister.

In Ghana, the word family is not limited to a simple conjugal pair of household children but rather a very wide circle of people. My uncle Kumah died early as a result his children were untrusted to my father. His household consists of numerous rooms that are occupied by his wife, nephews, cousins, and we the young ones. In those days, having more kids was the order of the day. Parents believed that a lot of children will provide them with more hands on the farm.

One thing they have forgotten is that plenty of kids will in a sense help on the farm, yet it means each person in the home has extra needs that cost money. The head of an African home is the man. He made all decisions and executed orders. My father was a disciplinarian and commanded respect from the whole family and his community. In Africa, you must have respect for elders whether you like it or not. An elder is an automatic leader irrespective of your level of education.

That was the type of house we were born into. We could ask or question our father about any issue provided it was in line with respect. Most of the time, our mother got all the required information from him for us. An African child who is learning how to grow has to divide his or her time between studies and household chores. If you really want to get the chance to go to school, then you must be prepared to abide by the rules of your father. You cannot just decide to go to school and that is all you would do. You have to be prepared to go to the farm as well.

My stepmother was the architect behind our success. She was the one that raised us. She really played the key role in our lives. My father did not tolerate any nonsense. A mere look at his facial expression could depict to you whether he was serious or not. He was a disciplinarian and a counselor. He did not want any bad nut or apple in the house. Even though he could not go to school to study formally, he had house knowledge coupled with a sense of wisdom.

Here is the biography of my father. Togbe Edward Kodzo Mensah Ankuvie was born in 1908. His father was Togbe Nanitor Yao Ankuvie (in private life) and mother was Mary Foli (all deceased) of Wusuta. He was of a noble birth, and he lived a noble man to his death. He did not have any formal education, but he was diligently tutored by his father, and brought up into the family of brave, honest, and hard-working men. With distinction, he learned the ways of a traditional man from his father.

In 1928, as the business of the time, he accompanied his father to Akposso of Kpete Bena in the Republic of Togo where the father acquired for him a large track of forest. He cultivated this land into cocoa farm which is part of his success story. Having established himself, he took his first wife who was the late Madam Lucia Dzato (maiden), and we are proud to say that they wedded before the church. He equally worked hard in the faith and rose to limelight in Kute as the Parish Chairman of the local Roman Catholic Church.

Between 1940 and 1982, he was at his enterprising best as a Purchasing agent for a number of Cocoa Marketing Companies, Manager of the farm hands on his cocoa farm, and a shop-owner who retail provisions. He started at Hohoe first as agent for the then UAC, until the establishment of the Cocoa Marketing Board. This brought to an end private participation in Cocoa Marketing in Ghana, thus cessation of that business.

He moved to Bena in the Republic of Togo. There again he secured agency with one French Company after another in purchasing cocoa. During this period, he built the house at Kute and opened a shop for retailing provisions. He also built the residence at home, and after the closure of the earlier store, he opened another in the building at home in Wusuta. It was through this venture that he suffered a major setback. His store full of wares were vandalized and sold off cheaply during the Price Control days in Ghana history.

In all his life, he exhibited sterling qualities of character. He was disciplined, peaceful, law-abiding, principled and not dogmatic, kindhearted but never found to sympathize with anyone who mismanaged his or her life. He cherished good things in life, worked hard, and was content with any condition of life. He was gentle, warm to everyone that approached him and a shrewd businessman.

To the family, he was the harbor to which all distressed ships berth. He helped many people in the family. Fo Mensah as the adults fondly called him, had ears for every troubled heart. He brought his self-disciple to bear on all those who surround him. As such, drew only the disciplined to him as a magnet. To his chosen, he taught out of his experience, the tenets of success in life. His ways endeared him to many people. At the time of his death in 1998, he was survived by two wives, eleven of his own, and eleven children of his deceased brother's (Kumah)entrusted to him. May the Lord grant him eternal rest! In French, Adieu!

We all followed the pieces of advice of our parents and looking back to those days. I can see the impact they have made in our lives. As I indicated earlier on, my father gave birth from four women and only my stepmother Nana was able to withstand the hard moments. She is popularly called as Mama Tokoe and Nana. She gave birth to Mawuse Pauline Ankuvie, Dr. Ankuvie Augustine, Paul Kwame Ankuvie,

Hellen Babe Ankuvie, Faustine Enyonam Ankuvie, and Philomina Nana Ankuvie.

I grew up to hear that "Behind any successful man, there is a woman." Her good intention for all kids without division was a clear manifestation and living testimony in relation to that wise saying. She raised a bunch of kids and anyone that listened to her was successful. She was a good listener and someone who shares the sentiments of other people. When we were growing in the village in Togo, I could remember one day that while playing, I was called to come and say hi to my biological mother.

I did not really understand it until I got there and was introduced to the woman that came to visit as my real mother. So, all along I was thinking that she was my actual mother just because there was no abuse, or any art of discrimination. She instilled the spirit of togetherness among everyone. We all performed the same amount of labor. Domestic chores, like fetching of water and firewood from the farm, sweeping the compound with a broom, cooking, and washing of dishes were equally distributed among all of us.

I went through class one to class six in Togo and spent two years at Wusuta in the Volta Region of Ghana without seeing my own mother coming to say hi. I moreover spent five years of high school at Kpando Secondary. The distance between the school and Anfoega-Dzana, where she was residing was less than twenty miles, yet my own mother could not take one day to visit me in the boarding house. Had it been for the works of Mama Tokoe, I don't think we would have been in position to make it up to this far.

Our father became weak somewhere along the line, but life must go on. We have to eat, clothes, and go to school. Through her home training, we all had a chance to set a fire, heat water for baths, cook breakfast, wash dishes, sweep, clear bushes for farming, planting, use of machete to cut branches of trees, carry water in a bucket or in a pot from the riverside, washing clothes, cleaning, and so on and so forth.

There was no abuse of children, nor greed. Her critical roles made it possible for us to have food and security all times. She ensured that we had enough to eat. A child that gets enough food to eat is bound to behave normally. I have seen so many abuses of kids by some cruel stepmothers back at home. Such women only made their stepchildren do all the cooking, cleaning, organizing and carrying numerous errands.

They did not give ample time to their step kids to study in school. Some children were either late or don't even get equal chance to go to school. Some women lavish expensive gifts on their own kids to the neglect of stepchildren. Step kids are warned not to tell anyone, otherwise they will suffer the consequences. Some instances show symptoms of abuse like scars and burns, human bite marks, etc. Some can tell you face to face "I am not your real mother" or "Do not call me your mother."

Such cruel behaviors of some stepmothers back at home in those days were much to be desired. Spanking and severe beating are some of the experiences of some kids. Begging or pleading fell on deaf ears. You can image the psychological impacts on such children. Whenever the father of abusive kids is around, everything appears to be normal. Once they are out of sight, the various maltreatment resume or continue. There is no closeness or family bondage between stepchildren and some guardians because maltreatment given to them. There is therefore conflict in the mind of abusive children. Nothing good the child does is appreciated. I am glad to tell you that my case was the total opposite.

Two or more kids who are returning from school, stepmother runs to hug her own without showing affection to other ones because they are not part of her blood. In most cases in Africa and elsewhere, probably the victim's mother is dead while the child is at a tender age. The father may remarry in the life of such a child who deserves tender love from a mother.

When you do good things to someone in life, you may be doing it for yourself or for your generation. Anything bad that you would do to someone will eventually come back to haunt you. I believe in cause and effect. If you dig a hole for someone to fall in, you may be the same person that will fall through. There is a price to pay for every bad occurrence. It is up to you to choose. A good stepmother's loving care is a typical manifestation of my life. I therefore urge you to stop the maltreatment or the abusive acts now!!

I believe you will agree with me that children that are often maltreated may grow to have negative impacts on them. And that will not be their fault to be wicked or to react negatively in society. They may appear to be normal but are somehow affected. The circumstances surrounding their life prompt them to be hostile instead of being friendly. They may appear to be normal but are not. They don't even have love for mankind. They don't have affection or a kindly feeling toward their fellow human being just because of cruelty or weakness they have suffered from their hosts.

It does not matter in life if it is your brother's or sister's child. The most important thing is that he or she is a human being. Some people are cruel to their maids or domestic servants to the extent of beating and molesting them. Some victims suffer from drowning, burning, lashing, bleeding, and cutting just to mention a few of them. These are all reckless behaviors on the part of some parents on their step or maid servants. There must be equal parenting. Show love, respect, and human compassion for your step kids.

I am sure all these behaviors are still going on back at home and elsewhere. A change of behavior by a cruel stepmother can put a smile on the face of an innocent child whose mother has died or as a result of a divorce. I Don't appreciate those women who are separated due to divorce and would not like to pay a common visit to see how their children are doing. If you and your husband are separated, so what? You still have a role to play in the life of your children. So, get up, buy, a few things from time to time, and honor them a simple visit.

Your mere presence is a morale booster. You don't have to possess enough money in order to do that. A word of advice is more than just necessary. Most of the time, these kids are intimidated to the extent that they can't even put up a smile or show eye contact. They are simply afraid and are constantly thinking whether they are going to be blamed again and again. Children of this nature, when grown and become self-reliant, that is where you would see family members and loved ones who should have been there or stood for them emerging from nowhere.

I hate my African people and anyone who exhibit such behaviors. Some parents would be talking proudly and pointing fingers -this is my daughter or son. Where were you when he or she was suffering? We need to be there for our sons and daughters. Sometimes, the pain and emotional suffering becomes too much to bear and to forget. Discrimination of all kinds is not the answer. These are my elder brother's sons and daughters. African mentality! When the going is becoming tough for your family member, instead of you helping, you rather turn your back to laugh. I have seen it all with my eyes when I was growing. So I know exactly what I am talking about.

My own people are guilty of that. The very person who would be sympathizing with you is the same person who would be laughing at you in his or her heart. The teeth are boldly laughing, but the heart is saying I wish you suffer the more. Maybe that is why some people say, "Your best friend is your secret enemy." Beware of people!!

In my case, Nana, as we called her, has done marvelously to the extent that I don't even know how to describe her. She provided us with a surmountable love, and nobody felt lonely, let alone think whether she was our biological mother or not. She never blamed anyone's mother or dared to mention that she was not my mother. Mama Tokoe and my father who did not go to formal school tutored us in the house to what we grew up to be today.

She interacted with everyone and offered us council whenever necessary. You can see clearly that she had time for all of us. You can communicate with her anytime you want but do not try to cross the line of respect. I cannot remember any day that I felt like being with my biological mother instead because there was always such a unique line of cordial relationship.

Mama had an incredible amount of patience for everyone that consulted her. There were difficult moments in those days in Akposso where we the children of Edward Mensah Ankuvie got frustrated, but Nana assembled us under one umbrella. She helped our father to educate us. By then, my brother Augustine was in the medical school. Paul was in secondary school form three and I was admitted in the same school in form one. Then Hellen in Vakpo secondary school and Faustine was behind her and finally Philomina, our last born. Such was our financial burdens, and our enemies were laughing at us.

She was always assuring us of a brighter future. She said it several times that things will be fine one day. I wish my father was still alive to witness it. I don't know but, if people die and can meet their loved ones, I am sure when she joins our father one day, she can tell him all that transpired when he left to be with his maker in 1998. May he rest in perfect peace. Adieu!!

This is for mothers and fathers who may end up in a divorce. You still owe your child or children your motherly responsibilities. Your job is not yet over. You still have to visit and check on your children. Do not forget about them because you find your new husband. You need to find out from time to time how they are doing. Do they have food to eat, clothes to wear, and money to pay for their school fees?

When they are in boarding school, take a moment to buy some items such as pens, uniforms, footwear, provisions to supplement the dining hall's food. Be concerned!!! A mere letter from you the mother and phone calls will greatly be appreciated.

Those days in the village, we were taught how to cook meals, clean, wash dishes, sweep the household compound, fetch water from riverside, and weed the cocoa farm with cutlasses. Difficult and frustrated days are always reminding me. So let your past experiences remind you of your presence state and the future. Do I want to mess up with my life and go back to the suffering? Oh, hell no!!

Some people forget about their suffering and mess up with their hard-earned future. You pray for the chance to come your way and it has come. Will you be stupid to let it go? This is food for thought for every individual. Reflect over it, even ponder, or do self-examination. You never know tomorrow, that is why it is good to get prepared today. You may fall from a storey building to a marketplace. Who knows!!

A friend in Britain spoke to me about how someone managed to bring his wife to the United Kingdom. This woman after she got all her papers, started misbehaving toward her husband who waited on her for five years. She will not even like to clean their room. She gets up and prepare food to eat but will not like to clean the kitchen with the excuses that she was getting late to work. When the husband complained, there was a problem in the house. She will pour insults on this guy.

Such women like any other person is looking for opportunity to get out of poverty in life. Look at how her new society is changing her behaviors. According to reliable sources, the woman used to attend church services back at home constantly praying for God to give her husband. When God has finally answered her prayers, that was how she paid back her husband. My friend told me that the husband has to wait for her for five years before she finally got her papers to join him.

Upon arrival and getting used to the new environment, she began to misbehave. She even told the husband that she was sorry to accept her hands in marriage now that she joined him. But when she was waiting for visa, her intonation was all sweet and palatable. You see how human beings are? It made me sick in the stomach when I heard this story from my friend in Britain. She has already forgotten about the number of years the husband had to wait for her. Moreover, all the money the husband spent on her to get to Britain was no longer necessary. So many years of someone's hard toil of labor is in vain, don't you think so?

This is a stab in the back. Basically, she used you the man from her country of origin to Western Country or America. She waited patiently to get her Social Security Number and Green Card, so she can stay on her own. Now she is bluffing, and the next thing is she wants to be on her own. At this point going forward, she does not need your services. You have helped her to achieve her aims. Or simply put, I just want to use you to get to where I need to be, I am right where I need to be. Stay away from me. To me, you are a thankless person. I can assure you that there is no blessing in such a behavior if you decide to take such a course. These are the reasons why a lot of people are suffering these days and cannot get a help. Perhaps God in Heaven sees and knows our dark hearts best.

You may not handle the chance given to you when it comes. That is why you are going through your present circumstances. Your mindset is a determining factor when Almighty God answers your prayers and you think that is all you need. And these are the very people who calls themselves Christians. They pray loudly and dance in church services for people to see them that they are Christians. They even sleep or have secret affairs with pastors and some church members in the name of brother sister in the church. When the answers to their prayers are not coming, they begin to blame God. But God in heaven who see in spirit knows what we don't know. Maybe that is why "Man proposes, and God proposes." It is a pity.

MY BROTHERS
AND SISTERS

As I mentioned earlier on, my father gave birth to twelves children from four women. The first woman who gave birth to three children to my father was popularly called Kumanor. She comes from the Republic of Togo. She is from Akposso tribe and based at the Ghanaian border town with Togo known as Kute. This town is where our father established himself with a provisions store dated back in 1960s. He built a compound house at Kute. He was one time a cocoa buyer for a company at Hohoe in the Volta Region of Ghana.

From the story I heard growing up, his house and provisions store at Kute was no joke. His first wife Kumanor gave birth to three children. They are my father's well-catered and sponsored children. By then, the nine subsequent ones were not born yet. They are Matilda Ankuvie, followed by Patrick Ankuvie, and Comfort Ankuvie.

Based on what I heard, my father was swimming in the pool of success when he gave birth to these three children. As a rich man of the time, he took the best care of his children. Kids in the same neighborhood wished they had the same or similar parental cares.

He was well respected in his community and as a result of his financial status in the neighborhood, he was chosen to be a leader in Roman Catholic church at Kute. Kumanor and her children are based at Kute. She passed away not long. We all the time have to pass through Kute in order to cross the border from Ghana to Akposso Bibi and Bena in Togo. That was our frequent route. You have to board commercial vehicles of the time (Bedfords) with a lot of dust from Hohoe in order to get to Kute.

Upon arrival to Kute, you need to continue your journey to Akposso Bibi on foot. Kute is a border town between Ghana and Togo. There was no road linking Kute to Bibi by then. Every Tuesday was the market day. Students even walked from Kute to attend the Roman Catholic Primary School in Bibi those days. It was a busy route with a flooded river to cross for market women and other users.

Patrick Kofi Ankuvie as my father's second born, became our senior brother. He was tall and a handsome man. He commanded respect and was liked by all of us. Pat for short as we referred to him, and my two elder sisters enjoyed the good moment of our father. They were very lucky ones. Some of us came to hear the story that my father was rich. As a son of a rich man by then, Patrick had everything at his disposal. He even told us how our father was really rich and we did not come at the right moment.

The journey from Kute to Akposso is done on foot in those day for some miles. There are a lot of cross border activities linking Ghana to Togo through these two towns. There are broken dirt roads that lead to more broken dirt roads in Kute Buem. It is a border town in the Jasikan District of Oti Region of Ghana. You must be ready to walk some distances to Akposso Bibi in the past. When you get out of the Bedford Trucks by then, you will be covered by dust all over your dress.

On your way from Kute to Akposso, there are always farmers, traders, market women, students from Ghana to Togo, and other users of the road. The marketing day for Kute is every Tuesday while the one for Bena in my area is every Friday. Early in the morning on Tuesday, farmers bring their various fresh products to the market center. Women traders determined the price of commodities to their advantage. Agricultural products such as yam, cassava, corn, plantains, water-yam, rice, maize, okra, and other fresh products are normally brought to the market. Animals such as goats, sheep, chickens, and fishes are all sold on market days.

My senior brother Patrick was by then attending Lolobi Seminary school. As a rich man's child, he was in the boarding school. He had everything a school child is supposed to have in order to concentrate on his studies. Our father had money when he was there as a student. He himself had several times spoken about how he enjoyed life at the time our father used to have money when he was in school. From the story I heard, he could not cope up with the seminary life. As such he completed his Secondary School at Hohoe.

He subsequently taught at Peki and worked at Tamale in the Northern Region of Ghana. He then left for Nigeria for some years. He stayed there and relocated to La Cote D'Ivoire (Ivory Coast). He used to visit home and go back until he finally decided to return home in 1987. He spent few years at home and found life unbearable, so he decided to travel again. This time, he chose to travel to the far Spain in 1990. In 1993, the family received a letter with some pictures from one of his friends informing us of his death in Zaragoza Barcelona Spain. He is survived by four children. May his soul rest in perfect peace.

The next woman who gave birth for my father is called Celina from Anfoega Dzana in the Volta Region. She too lived at Akposso. She gave birth to Moses Kokou Ankuvie. I stayed with him at Hohoe after I failed English Language in 1993 O-Level examination at Kpando Secondary School. He had a Lotto Kiosk by then and he was making a living out of that. He moved to Accra to struggle for better life. His hard work paid off and he settled in Accra with two drinking bars at Teshie Nungua. He felt sick in 2018 and suffered from a strange sickness which took him to his grave in 2018. He left behind three boys, a girl and their mother. May his soul rest in peace.

Mama Tokoe popularly known as Nana also gave birth to six children for our father. She managed to stay and raised the rests of the kids my father gave birth to from other women. Her first and second children all died. The third one survived and is called Mawuse. It is an Ewe word. Mawu is the word the Ewe people from the Volta Region use to call God. Mawuse means God has heard. It is like you are praying and you expect God to answer your prayers. And when it finally happens, the Ewe people say the Lord has heard your prayers (Mawuse).

She gave birth to three children: two boys and a girl. One attended Vakpo Technical School. The other began schooling at Anfoega Secondary and later transferred to Bishop Herman Secondary School. The only female went to the family high school which is Kpando Secondary. She further attended Mount Mary Training College. The same school I went to and was posted to Wa in Upper West Region where I later won the U.S Visa Lottery.

Dr. Augustine Komla Ankuvie directly follows sister Mawuse. He completed class one to class six in Togo and then my father brought him to Ghana with Moses Kokou Ankuvie who all attended Wusuta Hotor L/A Middle School. We all followed their academic path. Augustine passed Common Entrance Examination as a short cut to enter into Kpando Secondary School. He was the first person among my father's children to attend Kpando Secondary from form 1 to Upper Six.

After O-Level, he did six form in Kpando Secondary and one-year National Service. Among us, he was a gifted person in school. We the subsequent ones all attended Kpasec except Hellen Ankuvie who attended Vakpo Secondary School. Dr. Ankuvie excelled very well and got admission to the University of Ghana Medical School in Legon-Accra. He did seven years of studies by dint of hard work. I am proud to say that he now holds Master's in Medicine. Congratulations Dr. Ankuvie and more grease to your elbow.

He was first posted to Donkorkroam in Afram Plains Evangelical Presbyterian Hospital. Paul follows Dr. Ankuvie. He too attended high School at Kpando Secondary. He completed F1 to F5 and proceeded to Ho Mawuli Secondary School for A-Level studies. Hellen Ankuvie popularly known as Bebe follows Paul directly. She finished secondary studies at Vakpo and went to Dambai Teacher Training College. She too struggled a lot and today I am proud to say that she is a classroom teacher at Wusuta.

The next person that comes after Hellen is Faustine Enyonam Ankuvie. She equally attended Kpasec under the new Educational Reform Senior High School. She graduated from the University of Cape Coast. She is also a teacher in Alavanyo Senior High Technical School. Our father's last born is Philomina Nana Ankuvie. She attended school at Wusuta and got admission to the family preferred Senior High School at Kpando. She graduated and went to the University of Development Studies in the Upper West Region of Ghana. Educating all your children can put financial constraints on your parents yet it is an investment. The beginning was really rough for us, but we all made it eventually. That is what our parents did for us.

My mother is the last woman to give birth to my father after Mama Tokoe. She gave birth to two of us; me and a girl by the name Edith Yawavi Ankuvie. I am writing this book. I already told you a lot about myself. My sister Edith was loud as compared to me. We all grew up in the village. As the tradition of the time, when you complete class one to class six in Akposso Togo, our father will bring you to Ghana to continue your education. She did not do well in school in Togo and was not able to finish six years of school in Togo. Our father decided to bring her to Ghana to continue her studies at Wusuta.

While attending school in the village at Wusuta, she started misbehaving. Growing up as a teenage girl, she thought she was fully grown up and did not need the advice of our parents and guardians. Attending school and socializing with peer friends in town, she eventually became arrogant in the house. At the same time, she was performing poorly in school. She did not realize that our father was financially weak hence the need to take her studies seriously.

Imagine your parents who are uneducated yet are willing to help us to acquire formal education. Money was hard to come by and as a child, instead of humbling yourself to get what you need for yourself, you rather decide to misbehave and be arrogant. What would be your fate then in such a hard time? You will be left behind and that was what exactly happened to her. As a young boy growing up, I was paying close attention knowing well the financial hardship in which we were.

Any sign of disobedience was not going to help me to achieve my goals, so I humbled myself to the best of my ability. She was the opposite. She was insulting our parents. Even though I did not like it, there was nothing I could do to stop it. It got to a point where our father got offended and likewise our stepmother. We all realized in the house that somewhere along the line that she was listening to outsiders. These outsiders were the people who were against my father including us the children.

This was how the devil entered our house and set my sister against our father and my stepmother. She could not realize that she was being used. At times, no one could talk to her just because she will not listen. Sometimes I personally felt that if you advise her, she can go back to inform the enemy. Her behavior got to a point where our parents became fed up with her and gave her life to her to do whatever she likes. She gambled with it and nothing good came out of it. She became pregnant and gave birth as a teenager. That was the moment she needed parental help but to no avail.

You see what happens in life when you choose to disobey your parents? No blessing of course, and her situation got worse. While I was trying hard to acquire my educational goals, she was left behind. My father kept quiet to see what she could do on her own as a teenager. Not long, she got pregnant again and gave birth to the second child. Only God knew how she managed. Her situation got to another level, and she left the house to travel to Lome the capital of Togo for a better life. All these she was doing with the influence of outsiders as against the will of our father.

To cut a long story short, she fell ill and died in 1999. She left behind two children namely Kossi and Jennifer. May her soul rest in peace! After my mother left my father, she gave birth to two other girls who are Amosi and Evelyne respectively. Their father died and my mother remarry gain for the third times. She gave birth to Kossi and Joyce all from Anfoega Dzana in the Volta Region of Ghana. My mother's brothers are Kossi (taxi driver in Accra), Francis Koku (Teacher), and Kokuvi (professional builder based in Accra).

My younger uncle is called Kokuvi. He began as a carpenter, and I remembered how my mother told me that we are almost of the same age. I used to visit them in those days in Accra. Uncle Francis Koku was by then a part-time teacher moving from house to house to teach kids in order to earn money for living. They toiled hard growing up because they lost their mother at early stage. They were struggling with life in Abeka-Lapaz down to New Boy Town. Anytime I visited them during my secondary school era, the least they had was given to me. My mother's sisters are Comfort and Johanna.

I did not grow up to know my grandmother. I was told she was very nice woman. Most often, good people don't live a long life. From the story I grew up to hear, she had a mysterious accident at Anfoega-Dzana. My sister Edith's early tragic death reminded me of how the devil can enter into your house and use your own blood against you. A nice family who began in the village under the auspices of my stepmother was somehow broken by some evil ones when we got to Wusuta. When you dig a hole for someone to fall in, you may be the very one who will eventually fall in. If you are not the very one to fall in, it can be your own children.

When I was growing up, I observed how some people can pretend to like you while in the actual sense, they hate you and can be working secretly against you. In my local language -Ewe, it is said "Adu konu dome to levo." It means how the tongue laughs yet inside the heart is different or cold toward someone. It may be dark in that person's heart toward you. In other words, "your best friend is your secret enemy." So be aware of your friends including your so-called loved ones just because you may not know the bad nuts.

I don't know what you will gain in spoiling someone's life. My property still remains my own even if you have a power to destroy my life with any means at your disposal. The legacy of your brother or your sister remains for his children. It cannot be changed overnight. I will go on to emphasize that "Good name is better than riches." As mankind, let us continue to demonstrate that pure kindness toward humanity without any reservation.

Some good memories in Akposso and at Wusuta with our cousins and nephews are worth mentioning in this book. When my paternal uncle Kumah Ankuvie died, his children were entrusted into my father's care. Among them is the prominent cousin by the name Fo Prosper. He is based at Ho the Volta Regional Capital. At the time we were in Akposso Bibi in Togo, he was there with our father on holiday. His presence was felt every now and then. He was the one we the young ones were looking up to at the time as role model.

Everyone referred to him as "Fo Prosper." Fo is an Ewe word that mean brother. So, it is kind of saying my brother (Fo Prosper). He is jovial and approachable up to today. He was very close to our father. Whenever we heard the news that he was coming to celebrate Christmas with us, our mother used to buy all kinds of food stuff such as yam, cocoa yam, plantain, gari, beans, and cassava down in preparation toward his coming. The day he arrived, you could imagine the joy and jubilation in the village.

Fo Prosper and our late brother Patrick Kofi Ankuvie died in (Spain) were our seniors by then. Fo Prosper was fond of using some terminologies for our mother. He can say "mia tu gate" meaning on that day, we were going to eat yam slice. He was by then the storekeeper at Ho Regional Hospital. My brother Paul and I used to get his room ready whenever he was visiting home at Wusuta.

Another cousin by his name Bernard attended Anfoega Secondary and Ho Mawuli School. He was also regular at Akposso during holidays. The village was full of people in those days. Other cousins were Fo Yao, Fo Komla, Dada Adzoa, Vicky and Pa Kwesi. They are our only aunt's Tasi Bedu's children. Christmas was in a full session in the village while Easter celebration was the occasion for all of us to gather in my father's big house at Wusuta. Mr. Bernard is now working in Ghana International School in Accra. We had fun in the village and enjoyed every bit of it. One Brother Yao too was coming from Donkorkroam to visit us at Akposso and he still lives there up to now. He is a very jovial and funny brother.

Brother Yao is a businessman at Donkorkroam. Fo Mensah uncle Stone's son was visiting the village too. He spent some years with us in the village. Foster and Moses all left the village to Hohoe where Mensah learned how to drive and Fo Moses (died in 2018), learned mechanics job.

JOINING THE UNITED STATES NAVY

At the time I was working in downtown Chicago as an overnight housekeeper, I was also looking for other job avenues and an opportunity to further my education to university level. My new host Elikplim was sharing ideas on more payable and lucrative jobs to me. Most of the time, when I was off, he was working. We only met for few hours in the house. One day, he told me how he wanted to join the United States Navy but due to some reasons beyond his control, he was not able to make it. So, he asked me if I was willing to join. Frankly speaking, he was the one who shared the idea of joining the U.S. Military (Navy) with me.

He subsequently took me to the recruiting station. I thought of the idea throughout the night and was considering it. While I was watching TV in the house one day, I saw the United States Navy advertisement about how you can get tuition assistance and a GI Bill to finance your education in the service and also after you get out of the Navy. I became attracted because I wanted to further my education. On a few occasions, I made inquiries and visited one school in downtown Chicago to ask questions concerning admission into a university.

The answers I got did not motivate me and as a result, I was still shopping around for more ideas. Working in the U.S. Navy and going to school at the same time sounded nice to my hearing. At the same time, I was still skeptical and afraid to join. I then made a telephone call to my brother, Dr. Ankuvie by then at Evangelical Presbyterian Hospital at Donkorkroam to seek his opinion on this issue. He said to me emphatically that I should not be afraid but to gather courage and join. He further told me that some of his school mates were serving in the U.S. Navy.

Also, he said that it is a difficult job, but he knows that with sheer determination, I can do it so I should go ahead with my plan. With the encouragement from my brother, I told my friend host—Eli that I was ready to join the service. One day when he came back from work, I finally told him that I was ready to join U.S. Navy. Eli said that he will find time one day to take me to Navy recruiter. I shared the idea of joining U.S. Navy with some other people and they discouraged me from joining. They told me that once I join the U.S. Navy, I will be taken to war zone and die. In actual fact, when I was told that I was going to die, I became afraid. Something within me told me that I should call my friend and reverse my decision. One day when we woke up, he asked me to dress up so that we could go to the recruiter. I eventually got ready and we left the house to USN Recruiting District at FT Sheridan, IL 60037 Chicago. We were welcome upon arrival as if they were expecting us. The recruiter asked me some questions in an attempt to establish some facts. My school certificates from Ghana were reviewed and I was asked to take a pre-test as it has been the case.

I sat down and took the test. He marked the test and told me that if I study hard, I will be able to pass the actual test. He referred some books for me, and I went to buy them. He also made me to watch a movie about the activities of the United States Navy. I began to study toward the actual examination. My house address 1457 West Victoria Street, Chicago IL 60660-0000 was taken, and the recruiter started stopping by to see how I was doing once in a while. John was his name in paygrade E-5. I was also given some dates to show up at the recruiting station and go back home.

The day of the real examination came, and I was given a ride to the center to take it (Chicago MEPS, DES PLAINES, IL 60018-1960). A few days later, I received a telephone call from my recruiter congratulating me of passing the test. The following day, I went back to the station in order to start filling paperwork. My recruiter told me that I was going to start from pay grade E-3 and I did not even know anything about it. American paperwork!! It came to a point where I was getting tired of the process. Signing a lot of documents!! Finally, everything was good to go, and I was put on the United States Navy Delayed Entry program awaiting shipment to boot camp.

A date was set—the twenty-fifth of October 2000, I was departing to boot camp. I was enrolled for four years (MS) Mess Management in my contract after which I will proceed to Texas Air Force Base for my Class A School. Until I left to boot camp, my recruiter paid a regular visit to me in the house to see how I was doing. The final day came, and I left the house saying bye-bye to my brother Eli on the twenty-fourth of October. At the recruiting station, other people joined me. Later in the day, we were all taken to a hotel to lodge. The following day, a bus came to take us to the main office where we finally raised our hands to swear the oath of allegiance to defend the United States of America against all enemies, foreign and domestic.

Right after we raised the hand to defend America, we were asked to enter a big bus to the airport. At the airport, we met the actual bus to boot camp. Military orders started immediately at the airport. Yelling and shouting on us began as if we were slaves. So, on the twenty-fifth of October 2000, I arrived to the boot camp in great Lakes Illinois. Life was not easy for me at all in the camp. I did not like the atmosphere in the camp, and I hated everything I went through. Marching together to everywhere, drilling, swimming, and bad weather-my first experience with snow was not easy to cope up with in any way.

Upon arrival to the camp, come and see the real and actual military discipline. Who are you to talk back when orders are given out? All the civilian freedoms were stopped right at the airport where we boarded the bus. When we got to the camp, it was getting dark, and we were ordered to come out. We formed a line and followed each other into the processing building for new arrivals. We were made to understand that military training had begun in our life. The first thing I did not like was how we were stripped naked of our civilian clothes and given military dresses. No privacy was observed any longer. The civilian clothes everyone was wearing were parceled and shipped to our respective homes.

All the processes we had to go through in order to begin military drills were completed on time. Until then, we were kept in the building even in the night. I thought we were going to sleep and come back the following day, but that was not the case. Rather, we had to go through so many processes for some hours. We were being watched closely and if you were caught sleeping, you knew what was going to happen to you.

We went through such horrible processes and finally got every gear for our training. I was put in Division 026. If you don't have patience, I can assure you that by the time you go through boot camp, you will probably develop high blood pressure. I remembered how we were marched to barber shop and they cut our beautiful hairs with no exception. I was in boot camp in October when the weather was getting bad. Great Lakes Chicago and the snow weather!! I am sure you know how cold and chilly it is in that time frame. We were in line together to everywhere. It is only when you could not go through a program successfully and there is a need for you to go alone, that is when an individual is allowed to walk alone (strugglers). Otherwise, all the time it is about a teamwork. The ship sails with everyone onboard and we incorporate the same spirit in boot camp.

As soon as we arrived in boot camp, I started hearing terminologies such as the deck (floor), head (restroom). Time was not available for detail stuff. We are given time to shower, to eat in the chow line and to do everything. Imagine you are given five minutes to enter the small bathroom and shower. Come on!! We also had a wake-up bell early in the morning at four a.m. It is called 'Reveille and Reveille'!!! When you hear that it means you must jump out from bed and stand by it.

The instructors will go around to ensure that everyone was up. We were then given few minutes to make our bed (bunk) as was directed by instruction. Recruits as we were called in training, rushed to the head to brush our teeth in no time. We all dressed up in the uniform of the day and start following the plan of the week. We often go through some drills before lining up to march to wherever we were supposed to be.

When it came to marching, I often messed it up. Instead of moving my left foot first, I stupidly moved the right one. I therefore jumped it up and get embarrassed while marching. When it came to the actual military drills like push-ups, and sit-ups, come and see me struggling!!! I was not used to such bodily exercises. I couldn't stand it from the beginning but had no choice. I cried most of the time when it was time to go through them.

I did not like the fact that we have to line up in a group to march to everywhere. I thought of running away but I was not sure of how to do it. The snow weather did not favor me in anyway. I just came to the States on the fifth of July 2000 and joined the Navy on the twenty-fifth of October 2000. As such, I did not have any experience. I only saw snow on CNN back at home. But here I am today walking every day in the snow from early in the morning to evening. One day while still in the camp, I remembered how one of our instructors called me and took me outside to perform a snow angel show. Somebody told him that I was new to the weather. Some of my fellow recruits laughed at me while I was on the ground doing it. Whenever you hear the term recruit, you should know that they are referring to you. When you hear military order coming from the instructors, you need to come to attention immediately. Otherwise, you have to drop.

Dropping is used when you have to do some numbers of push-ups for an offense committed. Basically, when you fail to answer a question in the proper way be prepared to standby. When a simple order is given for instance to keep our mouths shut and listen, someone sometimes mess it up and we have to pay a price as a group by doing a number of push-ups. Also, when a recruit failed to execute a drill properly, the whole group will start up all over again. Such behaviors annoyed me all the time. I was never happy in boot camp. Almost every day, there was a new challenge I had to face.

One most outstanding one was how to qualify for swimming test. I thought it was easy to swim. I could not qualify the first time we had to swim. I was not able to float. I drank some water before I was rescued, and it was not an easy thing. It probably sounds funny to you because you know how to swim but I don't. It was an obstacle on my way. Do you know how many times I had to walk that long distance to get there and qualify? You can guess!!!

Not once, twice, but a number of times. If I tell you probably, you will end up laughing at me. Anytime I was coming afar, the instructors who have already seen me and know me perhaps expressed their frustration about me coming to disturb them again. I felt bad but I had to go in order to pass it and if not, I was not going to graduate on time. I kept trying but could not make it on time and I was transferred to another Division—046 for one more week. By then my original Division—026 already graduated and left.

My original division—026 was supposed to graduate on the twenty-ninth of December 2000. They did but I could not graduate with them due to some circumstances beyond my control. So, I was transferred to another one-046 if my memory can serve me well. Luckily, I ironed out all my differences and came out in the first week of January 2001. After boot camp, I proceeded to my -A School. Your Class A school is your direct job offered to you to do in the Military. Since I wanted to be a cook in the Navy, I had to go to San Antonio in Texas for the school. The school was located by then in an Air Force Base by the name Lackland. We had to attend classes with Air Force fellow members. It was a kind of USAF/USN Consolidated Food Service Course. The atmosphere in Texas was more civilian as compared to that of Boot Camp. I enjoyed this place better than Boot Camp. I became normal and like the A school.

While we were off during the weekend in A school, we boarded a taxi in a group to downtown San Antonio to walk around and also to enjoy the beautiful view of its River Walk. It is a tourist-attraction and it is much to be desired. Some people say it is the cultural gateway into the American Southwest. When you are there, you will not feel like going home due to sightseeing, shopping, food and a lot of fun.

The River Walk is all on a world-renowned 15-mile urban waterway. It is also known as San Antonio's treasure and the largest urban ecosystem in America. It equally provides a serene and a pleasant way to navigate the city. You can also explore the downtown River Walk by jumping aboard a river barge for a ride and a well guided tour. We had the opportunity to visit The Tower of the Americas and dined in the sky. The view is very magnificent and gave me a good memory of San Antonio while I was there for three months.

The Navy A school is where you go to learn about your specific job. I was by then assigned as MS-Mess Management Specialist School where you will learn how to cook, bake, and take care of the Ship's Galley. You will be cooking for your fellow shipmates and as such, you need to learn a bunch of stuff in order to execute your job more efficiently. That is why we have to attend class A school for such purposes. Some people wonder why as a cook, we have to go to school again to learn how to cook since it is easy anyway. Cooking and baking are arts that are derived from scientific research.

At Lackland Airforce Base in San Antonio, we the Navy students learned about the basics of cooking, baking and general sanitation practices. The job of cooking in the fleet requires us to learn how to manage a general Mess and a Private Mess on board the ship as well as Ashore galleys. In those days, we were called Mess Management Specialists (MS), and now we are noted as Culinary Specialists (CS). Our training program by then was consolidated between the Air Force and the Navy.

Part of our job requires us to take care of Navy living Quarters. We spent three months in Lackland Air Force Base and graduated in March ending. We have to stand quarter deck and security watches during the weekend. You have to pass every test in order to graduate. We take a test right after completing a chapter as part of continuous assessment.

Finishing a chapter and giving students few days to study for exams or tests was not the case like I was used to in Ghana. You better be prepared each time you enter the classroom. We left for classes in the morning and closed at four to five o'clock in the evening.

Although there were frequent intervals for smoke breaks, it was still an intensive academic program. I managed to go through the A School programs and on twenty-sixth of March 2001, I graduated from Lackland Air Force Base in San Antonio—Texas. I was so glad I made it by dint of hard works. I then took ten days of leave from the twenty-sixth of March to the ninth of April 2001 to return to Chicago—my home state in the U.S.

I was so happy that I finally came back home—Chicago since I left on 24th and went to Boot Camp on 25th of October 2000. That was why I missed home in uptown Chicago. My brother Elikplim was at the airport to welcome me. When you travel and it is time for you to come back and someone comes to meet you at the airport to pick you up, it really feels good trust me.

I narrated all my ordeals to my brother while he was listening but could not help it but to laugh at me. The way I struggled to do push-ups and sit ups was quite funny to listen to. How I cried in the course of going through everything was amazing and the reality on the ground as I began to settle in America. Getting the opportunity to travel from Africa to America and the Western countries as an immigrant with no family member to welcome me home directly was not easy. As a result, I had to do that in order to get my own peace of mind and I am proud of myself to do that.

MY FIRST DUTY STATION

After I left Lackland Air Force Base in beautiful San Antonio—Texas, where I graduated from A School on the twenty-sixth of March 2001, I went on leave up to the ninth of April 2001. On the tenth of April 2001, I checked in to my first Command USS Bridge AOE-10 which was based by then in Bremerton in Washington State. I flew from Chicago O'Hare airport to Sea-Tac airport with other shipmates also reporting on the same day.

USS Bridge is the naval ship which has taken its name after Commodore Horatio Bridge of 1806 up to 1893. According to history, Commodore Horatio Bridge served as the Chief of the Bureau of Provisions and Clothing for fifteen years thereby making a tremendous distinction to a comprehensive fleet supply. The motto of my first ship by then was "Service with Excellence." As far as I know, the mission of USS Bridge was "to provide fuel, ammunition, provisions, and store fleet freight, mail, and personnel via CONREP or VERTREP in support of fleet operation."

We were picked up at the SEA-TAC airport by the Navy duty van driven to Bremerton where the ship was stationed. The van dropped me in front of a Bachelor Living Quarter. I was told to go in to inquire information about my ship. A phone call was made to the ship's quarter deck and in a few minutes, the duty driver on that fateful day was sent to pick me up. The lady who was working at the front desk asked me to standby while waiting for the duty driver.

In no time, the duty driver came to get me. We then proceeded to the ship's yard with its top security measures. Finally, I carried my sea bag and climbed the ladder leading to the ship's quarter deck. Upon arrival to the quarter deck, the Officer of the Deck (OOD), asked me of my rate and few questions, I was told to wait for an MS to come from the galley (kitchen) to pick me up. He helped me carry my bag to the galley area and to the Chief's Office. Dinner was over by then. I was led to a deck below the galley. That was the Supply male berthing—our sleeping place.

The following day we went to quarters—Navy assembly for muster, inspection, and instruction. During quarter's, we are inspected for uniforms, haircuts, fingernails, and absolute personal hygiene. The Leading Petty Officer speaks, follows by the Chief, Senior Chief and Food Service Officer providing the necessary information to their Sailors. The Leading Petty Officer, mostly a first class, take charge of the division after the chief and any higher chain of command has spoken. Any newcomer fresh from school is introduced. That was the moment my name was mentioned, and I was welcomed into the Food Service Division. As a new arrival, you have to check into the various departments of the ship. So right after quarters, one first class took me around the ship to check in. When I finished checking in, I was issued cook uniform. No time to waste at all. Even though Culinary Specialists go to A School, we don't know everything until we actually start working in the galley aboard the ships. I realized I had to learn a lot in a fast way within a short notice.

We usually have two working groups and while one team is working, the other one is off. They are called Port and Starboard Watches headed by a Watch Captain. The Watch

Captain is the term that is referred to the one in charge of a working group. He is the one who assigns everyone a product to cook when that watch is working. He or she makes sure that the food is cooked and is up to proper temperature and ensures that everything is done accordingly.

As cooks of the ship, we are noted as the "heart of the ship." We make it to happen on the ship. We are the hot cakes on the ship because if you have to eat, you need to line up and wait for the serving time. Our job is a morale booster for the crew. We take care of food service on the ships and ashore galleys. The job of the cook is even extended to the White House for the President of the United States. Before the ship gets underway, it is the duty of the cook to order the required amount of various food stuffs that will be enough for a certain period of time.

We follow a nutritious and a balanced diet menu. We prepare, cook and maintain all galley equipment, and see to record keeping of food supplies. We cook, bake and maintain absolute control of sanitation of our dining areas. Part of our job is to take care of living quarters as well. The Mess Deck is the crew's dinning place, and the galley is called the General Mess. That is the kitchen where the food is prepared for the crew in pay grades E-1 to E-6.

Private Messes on the ship are that of the Chief Petty Officers, the Wardroom and the Commanding Officer's kitchen on small ship such as the supply ships. The Chiefs eat in CPO Mess. Officers of the ship dine in the Wardroom, including the Executive Officer of the ship. As cooks, we are rotated in every six months to man these Messes. I started as a cook on a watch. I did not know what was going on at first.

You wake up and come to work in order to be instructed. I was the last seaman who just checked in and it meant a lot at that moment. You will be dogged around. Other cooks will use you to accomplish their scheduled tasks. They don't care if you have a product to cook on time. Such was my situation. I will be cooking and before I realized, another person ahead of me will just come to instruct me to go and do another job.

With fear and intimidation of the time, I had no choice than to abandon my product and proceeded to carry out that instruction and come back to my original work. I can still remember a statement an African American made to me when I was coming from the bathroom the following day, I checked in. He wanted to know where I come from. A mere look at my face by everyone can tell that I am not born in the United States and my accent too. Everyone wants to ask you "Where are you from?" as a result of your accent.

I told him that I am from Ghana in West Africa. He said he was happy to meet me and to see an African in the U.S. Navy. He further told me that his time was up and was getting ready to come out of the service. He however stated that it sounds nice to see me as an African on the boat but in no time, I will actually find out what it means to come from Africa and be in the United States Navy. There was another guy standing by and rebuked him for what he said. But to him, he was being frank to me by just telling me the truth.

I did not get the message right from the beginning until somewhere along the line. He made me to wake up from my slumber and live up to my uttermost expectations. At my work center, for some reasons beyond my understanding, if you are an immigrant, it means you must act stupidly. We follow the same routine everyday by arriving to work at 4:00 am in the morning and start cooking breakfast. By 6:00 o'clock, we then start serving our Sailors and by 7:30, we shut down on the ship and on shore duty, we close at 8:00 am. And that should constitute our routines and an individual should definitely register it in his or her mind.

Because I am performing well and not acting stupidly enough to attract yelling, I have to face series of maltreatment. The issue I am expressing here was not a joke at all. I was tossed around very well. Some of our cooks picked quarrels with me for no apparent reason even though I could guess the answer. After going through fifteen years of education in my country and taught in classroom for three years, I don't know why I have to start behaving like a fool in the United States.

That reminds me of what I have been seeing on TV about my continent. I have to behave like a fool at work at the age of twenty-nine by then because I am from that part of the world that is shown on television networks as a place of diseases, hunger, poverty and the place for animals. It is good to be educated. I never thought of any negative thinking like that until I got here. It makes me sick in the stomach, but I left home, and I am now on a foreign land trying to make a living.

It came to a time where I was rotated to the bakeshop of the ship. The Petty Officer Second Class who was supposed to train me in the bakeshop just took me there and said this is the bakeshop and closed the door and left me there by myself. Basically, I have to figure it myself. No training at all just because I am an African junior cook who is smart. I had to read the recipes and followed the instructions on the cards by myself. I could not complain to my immediate supervisor because the PO2, the Watch Captain, the Galley supervisor, JOD supervisor, and the Chief are all from the same country and speak the same Language. Imagine me as the last junior African Sailor checking in not long.

I struggled initially and made some mistakes in the first month of being in the bakeshop. I had to throw some products away because they did not come out well. We had a giant and a tall African American Leading Petty Officer

(LPO), but I was afraid to approach him. After few weeks, my products in the bakeshop started coming out better and I became used to the struggles over there. The most interesting was that I was learning something new every passing day and I was improving upon each day. Not long I found out that the baking aspect is purely scientific and if you dare don't follow the various steps, your products will not come out well.

You can ignore certain information on the recipe cards when cooking in the Galley, but your products will come out with a nice taste. But you cannot do that in the bakeshop. As time went on, I became better with confident in baking and my dinner rolls were awesome. I started making cakes, cookies all from scratch whenever we did not have the frozen dough in the freezer. Some of my products for breakfast were coffee cakes, cinnamon rolls, muffins, classic croissants, doughnuts, apple fritters, kolaches just to mention a few. I made cakes, cookies, pies, and rolls for lunch and dinner.

When I made PO3, I was assigned to the Commanding Officer's galley under the supervision of my mentor who later became a Chief. The CO of my first ship (USS Bridge-10), by then was a female. I did that job with a lot of caution. Cooking for one person sounded easy. The Commanding Officer ate small portion of food. The bad report I had from my supervisors while I was serving the CO was that I fed her with too much food than required. I did that for a month and was brought back to the bakeshop again. I spent much time in the bakeshop and earned recognition and a lot of accolades from the crew of the ship. Anytime the ship was at sea and we were doing underway replenishment, we have to make fresh cookies for an exchange. I was in bakeshop during September 11, 2001, popularly called 9/11. 9/11 attacks were a series of four coordinated terrorists attack by the militant Islamist terrorist group Alqaeda against the

United States on the morning of Tuesday, September 11, 2001.

It came to a time, and I was rotated from the bakeshop to the Wardroom to cook for the Officers of the ship. It is the place where all officers come to dine and relax after a long day's work. The Wardroom is also used for all official ceremonies on board the ship. The Executive Officer sits as the head of the table while they all eat. Until the ship was decommissioned, we the cooks used to assist in food preparation at the general mess before bringing it to serve the officers in the Wardroom.

Those days, when an officer was about to be transferred to another ship, we had to prepare a big meal as a farewell in his or her honor in the Wardroom. Such meals require series of preparations. Dinner tables are set in a grand style. The menu was full of salad, soup, the main course, and the dessert as the last item. We normally have steak, lobster, and crab legs on special occasions. Anytime we were about to cook them, the news will be all over the ship and the crew love every bit of it.

I really found out that the cooks are the "heart of the ship" because when it is time to eat, we are always ready. A look in the eyes of fellow shipmates can depict to you that they are actually hungry. Even though it is not easy to feed such a large number of people. When I sit down and recollect those difficult moments, I have a feeling that we did our best. If my memory can serve me well, the crew number to feed was around five hundred. The Chiefs were perhaps thirty-six and about forty Officers.

My first underway was a journey to Cabo San Lucas in Mexico. When you immediately check on board your ship and it is getting underway, be ready to experience what is called "sea-sick" and that was what I went through. Some people also called it as motion sickness. As the boat is moving you will be feeling dizzy and vomiting up too. It is better you are around the restroom (head) so that you don't end up throwing everywhere in the galley.

The journey was rough because of the sea sickness but I forgot about it in a couple of minutes in Mexico. It is stressful on the boat but as soon as the ship pulled in for a visit, that was it!! We had fun upon fun!! All your worries will be gone until the ship will be getting ready to go back to sea. Underway the ship goes is the phrase you will hear when we pull out to sea. They make all kinds of announcement before we are allowed to go out. The worst of all is when you find out that you have to work upon arrival while the rest of the ship is going on liberty. I tell you what, it is a pain in the ass!!!! For we the Culinary Specialists, once we are done serving dinner and the duty supply comes to inspect our spaces to ensure that it is well cleaned, we can still go out every night until the ship go back to sea.

It is only the duty section members that cannot go out on the day of duty. If the ship will be in port let say for four days, one group (Port Watch) will be off for two days and come back to relieve another group (Starboard Watch) and vice versa. Guess where we usually go to have fun? All the good places in town such as strip clubs, disco, and where the ladies are. We work hard on the boat while it is underway so when we pull in, it is no joke we really have fun.

As Sailors, we get lap dances, and we head to disco to shake our asses. Ladies are all over the town because the news often spread that an American ship is coming or is already in town. The port call in Mexico was very memorable. After Mexico, we cruised back to the ship's homeport -Bremerton in Washington States. We came back and not long ago; we were told to get ready for a possible long deployment. You already know what happened on September 11, 2001? Imagine joining Navy on twenty-five of October 2000. Coming out of A school in 2001 just to experience unannounced extended deployment of 9/11.

I remembered a few days after September 11th attack and how the Commanding Officer assembled all of us on the fly deck with the news of a possible extended deployment. The CO of the ship made it clear to us that we should get ready as a combat-supporting ship, since we are going to play a crucial role in the war. I became afraid and did not know much of what was going to be next. The real time came, and we were deployed in Operation Enduring Freedom. I did not understand the real Navy I joined until we began the deployment. It was full speed of work each day to feed the crew and Air Crew till midnight.

The moment came and we were deployed to the Gulf. As Cooks, we worked for longer hours when we are at sea. By four a.m, we are already in the galley to assume morning work in order to relieve night crew. You have to be on time and not five minutes after four o'clock. You don't want to be late and get punished. Punishment for being late to work for the first time is verbal. A repeated action will lead you to paper counseling. Any serious disobedient act or poor performance can land you to report chit. When you are put on report, you are gradually on the way to Captain's Mast. It is also called the Commanding Officer's Non-Judicial Punishment (NJP) for short. At NJP, you will appear in a sharp uniform escorted by the ship's police called Master At-Arms and then appear before the CO. The captain stands and administrates justice. Anybody found guilty is punished severely. Some of the punishments arising from the NJP are reduction in rate and pay-grade, restrictions, extra military instructions, etc. If you don't want to get in trouble, you have to be very cautious. We are in a military for twenty-four hours a day and seven days a week and as such, you have to be careful. Any misbehavior is subject to punishment.

After feeding the crew breakfast, lunch and dinner, then all the Culinary Specialists and Food Service Attendants begin to clean the various spaces we own. We can spend three hours and over to clean the galleys. Our vigorous cleaning is called field day and it is a deep cleaning. During field day, we bring all food items out to the Mess Deck and thoroughly clean our spaces. After that we standby for inspection. Our Chief and Senior Chiefs bring a bright flashlight during inspection.

The first country we visited during the deployment after 9/11 was Hong Kong. It is a beautiful country and we had fun while over there. I did some shopping while we were there. We were in night clubs and the news were all over the town that United States ship is in town!! We normally go out in a group of two to four and at most five due to security reasons. American military personnel are not welcome in every country we visited. And that is why the buddy system is enforced to help us in time of trouble.

From Hong Kong, the ship went back to sea for hard work. Just like we have fun to the fullest, the same way we do the work too. Replenishment at sea continues. After a long underway, the MWR organized steel beach picnic as a morale booster for the crew. Ice cream special too dropped frequently. We celebrated Thanksgiving, Christmas, and New Year at sea in a grand style.

We are cautioned to go to outstanding and popular restaurants including night clubs for security reasons. You know how it goes with Sailors!!Once the ship pulls in, we are eager to go out and get drank. If you get into trouble during a port visit, you are likely to be put on restriction depending on your case. I love my freedom so much that I don't want to go through that. As a result of that everywhere we visited, I was mindful of my actions. I did not drink too much to the extent of getting drank and showing up to work late.

Everywhere the ship went I enjoyed the food of that country. Some countries don't have a drinking age limit as it is the case in the United States. That made it possible for a lot of Sailors to drink and I had fun in Singapore. As part of deployment toward Operation Enduring Freedom, we went to the horn of Africa to provide some logistics support to other ships which were conducting operations in that area.

It came to a time when we have to cross the international date line. A ceremony was organized in order to usher all the first time Sailors like me. It was not mandatory but almost everyone participated. It is a naval initiation rite. It commemorates a Sailor's first time of crossing the equator. In those days, it was noted as crossing the line. Sailors on the boat who have already passed through this ceremony are noted as Shellbacks. They are the Trusty or the Sons and Daughters of Neptune. Those who are about to go through the ceremony are referred as the slimy or pollywogs.

This day is full of activities and after the ceremony, no one goes back to work except the culinary specialists who are in charge of cooking the food. During the ceremony, Sailors who have gone through the crossing of the line already gather to take over all activities. We are forced to pass through a series of physical tests. A day ahead of the ceremony, they will gather all kinds of sauces to form a smelly mixture of hot sauces. Mostly, we combine soy sauce, vinegar, tabasco etc.

The smelly mixture of sauce is then poured on each individual's dress. On that day, you don't wear a nice dress just because you cannot wear it again. I remembered we were led to the flight deck and ordered to get down on the deck. We also crawled on our hands and knees. While one is crawling on the knees, they will pour water on you with a fire hose. At another station, you will be asked to kiss the royal baby's big belly which is coated with the mixture of sauce. Just after the initiation rite, you have to throw the dress you are wearing away including your footwear. Once you cross the international date line, you gain another day. That is to say that today becomes the day after tomorrow.

Once everything is done, we are issued a certificate to indicate that you are now a shellback. In the course of 2001 deployment, we visited Bahrain and Dubai (U.A.E.). Bahrain is very expensive. I was particularly pissed off how the exchange rate was at the time of the visit. I remembered how I gave U.S. one hundred dollars and just got thirty-seven Bahrain dollar.

We pulled into the US Base in Bahrain which is not far from Al Manamah the capital of Bahrain. The base in Bahrain is the Headquarters for the Navy's Fifth Fleet activities. That is to say -the Naval Forces Central Command. We spent few days and went back to sea. I enjoyed Dubai among all the countries the ship visited. In my point of view, Dubai is the next United States. It has developed into a large economic boom. In Dubai, my ship was in Fujairah and Jebel Ali respectively. I enjoyed Jebel Ali as compared to Fujairah. I admired the numerous infrastructural developments in Dubai as compared to my country Ghana. My country is blessed with natural resources such as Gold, Crude Oil, Manganese, Diamonds, Bauxite, Iron, and Cocoa.

The ship proceeded to Australia where we had a stopover in Perth and Fremantle. Fremantle is a few minutes train ride from the South of Perth City center. History teaches that it was once the gateway to Western Australia. It possesses a great working port with old buildings. There are a lot of tourist attractions in Fremantle. Some of them are Fremantle maritime museum, shipwrecks gallery, the cappuccino trip, and Fremantle market.

Perth is another great place to visit when you are in Australia. The capital of Western Australia is Perth. It has a train system which enable easy movement around. There is also Double-Decker Buses for city tours. Some of the places to visit include Swanbourne and Scanborough beaches, Perth Zoo, in addition to King's Park. It has other tourist attractions as well as night clubs. As Sailors, we always look for interesting places to visit in order to have fun whenever the ship pulls in.

We really had funs in Perth Australia and every Sailor who has been there before knows what I am referring to. To me personally, Australia has been the best port call we have visited while stationed on USS Bridge. After spending a few days at Perth, the ship left for Melbourne, the second largest city of Australia. That city is beautiful with a lot of tourist destinations. After Melbourne, we started heading home. Anytime we are deployed, and the time is due to go home to U.S., we have to pass through Hawaii in order to pick up family members.

It is a program called Tiger Cruise where a family member is allowed to fly to Hawaii ahead of time in order to join the ship on our way back to the ship's home port. Under this program, you cannot bring your wife or your husband on the ship. By the time the ship arrives to Hawaii, everyone who signed for the Tiger Cruise is briefed ahead of time with rules and regulations. When the ship finally arrives to Hawaii, come and see us jubilating!!! We are basically back to the shores of America after a long and hard deployment. Those shipmates whose family members will be riding the ship with them normally assemble at the pier to welcome their Sailors. Hawaii is a fantastic place to live. USS Bridge pulled into Pearl Harbor the Naval base in Hawaii. The shipyard is very significant to the United States of America if you can recollect the Japanese attack on the U.S. on December 7, 1941. It was the calculated and "surprise aerial attack by the Japanese upon American Pacific forces." The base is located on the South coast of

Island of Oahu. It is five miles east of downtown Honolulu and some miles east of Waikiki Beach.

Pearl Harbor is noted as "a major homeport and pit of the Pacific for U.S. surface ships and Allied of Pacific fleets." It is very beautiful. Honolulu serves as the capital town of the state of Hawaii. It is also described as "the sheltered bay" or "place of shelter." It has numerous tourist attractions such as the USS Arizona Memorial, and Bishop Museum just to mention a few.

At long last, the ship loaded all the family members in Hawaii and we were on the way home to Bremerton. Some shipmates are allowed to take leave upon arrival to Hawaii in order to make way for Tiger Cruise members. Tiger Cruise is the U.S. Navy sponsored program of family members and friends of the crewmen coming aboard the ship to see the job we do on the boat. The ship becomes full when we depart Hawaii. It means we the Culinary Specialists have extra mouths to feed. That is another challenging and busy moment for us, but we make it happen.

When Tigers arrived on the ship, they are assembled in the Hangar Bay, Mess Deck, and Wardroom for briefing about the way the boat operates generally and in the event of fire outbreak, where they need to gather at. This is done further through touring the spaces of the boat in order to get them acquainted in case of security measures and fire outbreak. I observed how some elderly tigers had difficulties in climbing the ladders and stairs of the ship. Even myself, I don't like the stairs of the boat. As cooks, we have to receive stores several times climbing the ladders down to the jack of the dust.

The tigers have the opportunity to witness the Navy air power demonstration after getting underway from Hawaii before all the battle groups made their way finally to the ship's homeport. If my memory can serve me well, the USS Bridge was attached to the USS John C. Stennis battle group following the September 11, 2001, attack. The air power demonstration is to show the skills and strengths of the U.S. Navy pilots launching and recovery methods of the various aircrafts onboard the carrier battle group. It is very nice occasion, and some tigers think that life aboard the ship is joyous all the time.

Tigers also had the opportunity to see the Navy's man overboard as well as general quarters drill popularly known as GQ. Man overboard is done on the ship to prepare the rescue team for real-life situations. In this type of drill, the ship's general alarm system sounds to signal the commencement of the drills. As soon as you hear the announcement, you need to muster at station.

We the cooks often muster on the mess deck for the drill while some go to muster at the lockers to don firefighting uniforms in order to fight the fire. The man overboard drills also proceed the GQ. It is mostly a time-sensitive design to find out how much time will be used to rescue a shipmate in a life-threatening situation. During muster time, the entire department takes roll of their Sailors to ensure hundred percent accurate accountability of their people. Fire drill is also conducted from time to time. In the course of this event, the crew wears fire protective gear. It is scary sometimes.

On the 28th of May 2002 by the grace of God, we made it to our homeport in Bremerton successfully. It was not easy West Pac, but the USS Bridge brought every Sailor back safe and sound. That reminds me of the motto of the ship "Service with Excellence." The ship does everything professionally taking into account all its safety precautions. Even though there were a few casualties, the overall atmosphere was safe and friendly. The morale was at its top level, and we came home with significant smiles at long last.

Home coming has been a long anticipation for every Sailor on the ship. When we are a month away to return home, we started counting the number of days left. Some enthusiastic Sailors even marked the number of days left on the calendar or on the assignment board. In the galley office, we had it marked somewhere. The next day, when we go to work, someone will erase the previous date and indicate how many days are left. Such a thing continued anxiously until the day we arrived.

I wish you can witness the ship's arrival moment at the ship's homeport after a long deployment at sea!! It is a very emotional time in the life of every Sailor. Family members are duly informed that the ship is coming home on that fateful day. By the time the ship pulls in, they are already waiting impatiently on the pier. The various media representatives in the area were there to cover the event. It is a busy day with a lot of traffic. The crew mans the rill. Meaning Sailors lining up on the deck of the ship in well-dressed uniforms usually dress blue or dress white.

Upon arrival and when the ship pulls into the dock, it is announced on 1MC which is the ship's announcing system all over the ship. You will hear the phrase which normally says, "moored the ship goes." What a joyful and emotional moment for us!!! However, we still have to wait for the brow—the long ladder which enables us to get on and off the ship. Anxiety of the long-awaiting family and the Sailors keeps on growing. You can see anxious Sailors looking around for their family and love-ones. Tears even come out in the eyes of both family and shipmates.

At such particular moment, all anticipation of home coming finally turned into excitement, and joyous occasion with children rushing to the returning parents followed by the warm embrace and kiss of the united families. Those of us who did not have anybody to welcome us are left to walk out of the ship lonely to our cold and dusty apartment. I don't even know how to describe such feeling. I just had to accept it in good faith. Imagine you don't have anybody coming to welcome you at the pier. As said earlier on, such single Sailors go home alone to a cold and dirty room which has been closed for over six months. That was my case in point. I had to swallow it like that with a lot of stress and what have you not.

When the brow is eventually opened, the Commanding Officer and some designated Sailors come out to kiss their wives. They are followed by some Selected Officers and enlisted Sailors. The media covered it all the way. Sailors will continue to come out in that order until everyone is permitted to depart the ship. It is a very significant moment in the life of every Sailor. On that day, the base will be full of traffic.

Since I did not have anybody to welcome me, I managed to endure the loneliness and took a taxi home. You can imagine how dirty my room was after locking it for over six months. It was cold since I cut off the power supply before I left as a way of saving some money by the time I come back from deployment. Most of the time, when we come back from deployment half of the crew go on leave. It is called stand down. We are given the same privilege during Christmas and New Year holidays to take two-week leaves in turn.

Somewhere in September 2002, we had a Command change and spent quite some time in homeport. Right after the new Captain took over the command, we went back to sea for our regular sea trials for fleet readiness. In March 2003, we were deployed again. The ship sailed to Maui in Hawaii. This time we were deployed with Nimiz battle group to the fifth fleet.

My ship had the opportunity to visit Jebel Ali in the United Arab Emirates. This particular deployment was toward Operation Iraqi Freedom. We had so many port visits in Dubai. The next country we visited was Singapore. The ship left Singapore and made a stopover at Hawaii. As usual, the ship picked up tiger cruise members and came back to Bremerton on the fifth of November. Bridge left her homeport in March and returned in November 2003. We spent eight good months at sea.

Bridge made her last port visit to Victoria in Canada before it was decommissioned. We were in a popular night club to shake our asses off as usual. While we are at sea, we communicate through email and few phone calls with the help of an AT&T telephone card which is sold in the ship's store. The boat often stops over at Manchester Fuel Depot for fuel. I have witnessed a burial at sea onboard the ship that appeared to be strange to me. But such is life. I understand that it is the wish of some Sailors and other people to be buried at sea.

That was the first time I heard that burial takes place at sea voluntarily. Before I joined the Navy, I did not know that the ship uses some terminologies. For instance, we refer to the floor on the boat as deck and the restroom as the head. Our wake-up call is known as reveille and even if you don't like it, you have to wake up. You cannot escape it. The only exception is when you work in the night and have to sleep during daytime. Also, when you have a medical chit authorizing you to be in bed. We call it (SIQ), meaning sick in Quarter's.

I have been sicked several times on the ship and I wished I was in civilian world. Guess what? When you are sick on the boat, you have to go to medical for ckeck-in. If your temperature is normal, you will be given some pills and go back to work. When the ship is in port, exactly at seven o'clock in the morning or seven thirty, you will hear on 1MC "liberty expires for all hands." Meaning that you have to be at work by that time. In that case, your freedom to depart the ship voluntarily is over until it will be determined by your department later in the day when work is done satisfactorily around fifteen to sixteen hundred military time. Another term we often hear on the ship is sea and anchor. You will hear it whenever we are about to get underway. The anchor is used to stable the ship in rough time at sea.

Whatever is done when they set sea and anchor detail, I don't know to tell you. My job is in the kitchen or in the galley as often referred to in the ship. When the brow is removed, you will hear three whistles on 1MC "underway the ship goes." Officers call is announced for them to muster with the CO. The crew assembly is called quarters. We go to muster for instruction and inspection. You will normally hear "quarters, muster, instruction and inspection. You better be there on time and in a clean uniform with your boots shining, well shaved and fingernails trimmed.

In port and when the ship is about to go underway, you will hear the term working party and that is having Sailors from all the departments of the ship to help bring stores onboard or offload. Sailors for Working party are often mustered in the Hangar Bay of the ship and led to the Mess Deck and the various storerooms especially for food service. When you hear flight quarters, it means the helicopter is about to fly. You need to stay away from that area.

Other frequent announcements on the boat to include sweepers, eight o'clock report which is done in the Wardroom, divers on the side, security alert, taps, secure at sea, etc... Sweepers is a call for the duty section to sweep and clean the designated areas, as have been the case. In the case of sweepers, this is how it goes "Sweepers and Sweepers! Man, your broom. Give the ship a clean sweep down both fore and aft, sweep down all lower decks, ladder wells and passageways, dump all garbage in the dumpsters provided on the pier." You have to carry your trash all the way on the pier when the ship is in port. At sea, all trash is sent to a designed trash room. That room stings like a hell!!

As a Culinary Specialist, when the ship pulls into a port, we have a lot of trash to throw on the pier. I can assure you that no one goes anywhere until it is all taken care of. That is a typical moment I don't like but that is the nature of the work. I cannot stand it but that is the nature of the work. If you really want to go on your liberty, you have to cooperate and get it done. Otherwise, you will not be allowed to go anywhere.

Divers over the side means there are divers over the side, do not rotate screws, cycle rudders, or take suction for or discharge to the sea or operate any underwater equipment without first contacting the chief engineer or the diving operator." At ten o'clock in the night, onboard the ship, they will make an announcement in this way "taps" meaning it is time for all lights to be off. All lights out!!All hands return to their bunk and maintain silence about the deck. Taps!! This is just to inform the crew that it is time to go to bed. It is very interesting how the ship has her own terminologies.

As a Sailor, you stand the chance of getting all kinds of health benefits ranging from medical, psychological and to dental. Once a member of the US Military, you are automatically enrolled in Tricare. Not only do you get medical care, but also your family members. Sometimes you have to pay a little amount of money for the sake of your dependents. You can even be away on deployment, but the Navy will still be taking care of your family. It is very expensive to foot your own health care bills in the United States. So when you consider the hard work in the Navy, you must not forget of free medical care and other benefits such as the GI Bill, and tuition assistance. The two can help you to finance your education to a higher level.

All said and done, on the twenty-fourth of June 2004, the Bridge was officially decommissioned and handed over to MSC. It is now under civilian control known as military sealift command. The USS Bridge is now called the USNS Bridge. The ceremony witnessed the passing of the commissioning pennant lowered to the outgoing CO who in turn, handed it over to the incoming CO. Having done that, the ship was pronounced decommissioned.

I remembered how we disembarked the ship in our sharp looking dress white uniforms to show that the ship has been transferred to Military Sealift Command. On the twenty-eighth, which was the last day set for everyone to vacate the ship. I gathered my bags and left the ship. I missed it very much. I first came onboard Bridge with a little idea as to how to perform my job as a cook. But with time, I picked up from my senior cooks and learned a lot from them.

I made a lot of unforgettable friends while I was on board the boat and made some observations as well. When you go to a new place, you will never know what is in store for you. I met one notable Supply Master Chief. He took care of all Supply Sailors. He prevented a lot of Sailors from getting into trouble and others who could have gone to the Commanding Officer's non-judicial punishment.

He attached values to all the people who were working for him. I also saw the difference as soon as he left the ship. The next person who imparted me positively on the ship was the Food Service Officer. He was the one leading the division when I checked in onboard the ship. He led the division very well and was very approachable with listening ears.

Another gentleman on the ship by then was the Assistant Supply Officer. He was a soccer fan. I observed the way he took time from his busy schedule to walk around asking shipmates how they were doing. He got out of the

Navy before the ship was out of service. He often visited the bakeshop where I was working at to see how I was doing. He several times came to my aid on the ship. I appreciated everything he did for me while he was onboard the USS Bridge.

At the time I first checked in, my division had a Senior Chief and Food Service Officer. He later retired from active duty. He was a good man. The Chief cook was from Philippines. This reminds me how the Food Service Division is dominated by the people from the Philippines onboard the ship. They occupy the Food Service Department in every ship in the West Coast. One thing I observed about them is that they are hardworking. He later left to teach in A - School at Lackland Air Force Base in San Antonio in Texas. The second chief who came to replace him was a black female. She took over and led the division until it was decommissioned.

My mentor was a First-Class Petty Officer. Had it not been his personal intervention in the division, I don't know what would have happened to me. He was the leading Petty Officer of the division until everyone was transferred to his or her next duty station. He left for San Diego and became a Chief. As a beginner in U.S. Navy in those days, I was faced with so many challenges which I did not anticipate. I faced tough discrimination within the division which was real, and I had to battle my way out.

He was there to encourage me to start speaking out because I was very timid. He gave me the words of hope that there will be a better future. I began on the ship as a seaman from the bottom (MSSN Ankuvie). It was not a joke at all. I faced series of discrimination at my work-place almost every day. Little did I know that I came from Africa the part of the world, which was regarded as the land of diseases, poverty, war, and where people live on trees. For such reasons, I have to be stupid at work just because my face, look, and accent, I have to be that person who does not know anything, and I have to be taught everything. He took care of me through those hard moment and I have been thankful ever since.

Contrary to such assumptions, I came to the United States after going through fifteen years of education as a French teacher in Junior Secondary School in Ghana West Africa. The certificate I had before I came to America was equivalent to the United States high school diploma, completion of three years of undergraduate work in elementary and lower secondary education, finally completion of additional undergraduate work. Educational Credentials, Inc. reviewed my certificates from Ghana. (http: www.ece.org).

Some of my fellow cooks onboard the Bridge were Nadege, Xavia, Nathaniel, Waddell, Stanley, Nabil just to mention a few. My regular liberty buddies were from Nigeria and Morocco. You have to find your people everywhere you go in life. My African brothers on the Bridge were from Togo, Nigeria, Ghana, Senegal, Cameroun, and Morocco. Other friends were from Jamaica and Haiti. We go out whenever the ship pulls in at a foreign port. The Moroccan later got out of the Navy to further his education.

Another fellow Ghanaian who used to be on the ship until he transferred to Japan was from Accra. The two of us were liberty buddy in Canada when the ship visited Victoria. There was another guy from Cameroun who plays soccer. He was out of the service in 2004. The other three regular friends I had were from Nigeria. One became BM1 and had to be medically processed out. The other one was electrician and he also got out. The third one taught me how to drive. He equally got out of Navy and joined Reserved. While he was in Reserved, he made chief and is now an Officer. Even though we left the ship in 2004, we are still in constant touch with each other and sharing mutual ideas as brothers who travelled from the shores of Africa for a common goal. They were Nabil, Demola, Frank, Stanley.

The last person who inspired me the most onboard the ship was my last Food Service Officer. He led the division at the time of decommissioning. He is a well-articulated individual and commanded respect to the uttermost level. He was always advising Sailors to pursue further education.

I personally took his words into consideration and began a degree program with Colorado Technical University online in 2004. I am proud to say that I have finished it and now hold a Bachelor of Science in Business Administration with a concentration in Management. May God bless him for his self-devotion and personal interest in his fellow Sailors. I could not forget about PC1. He helped me in various ways. We constantly had conversations on the passageways. He made Chief and after the ship was decommissioned. More grease to his elbow!!

MY SECOND COMMAND

I received new orders to USS John C. Stennis CVN-74 right after the USS Bridge AOE-10 was decommissioned. Stennis was by then stationed in San Diego in California. When I departed Bridge for the last time, I went on one month leave before checking onboard USS John C. Stennis. By then the ship was in deployment to the Pacific Ocean. Toward the ending of my leave period, I flew from Bremerton to TPU (Transit Personnel Unit) in San Diego CA.

TPU ensures that Sailors who intend to separate or discharge from active duty to civilian life do so smoothly. It also ensures that other Sailors in the transient pipeline get to schools and fleet assignments. While I was in TPU with other Sailors who were waiting for Stennis, we frequently had a brief about the whereabout of the ship at sea and the exact moment we can be flown to meet her.

One minute we are told to muster for possible information about our individual flight and in the next minute, you will be told to disregard the previous news given to you due to schedule changes. Some of us were assigned to barrack jobs while awaiting shipment. I returned from work one day to get the news that I will be flown the following morning so I should get my stuff ready.

The following morning, inspection was conducted for me, and my room was inspected. Most of the time, some Sailors don't take their time to clean and take their trash in their respective room. The duty van took us to the airport in San Diego to catch the flight to San Francisco to Japan—Okinawa, where the helicopter flew us onboard USS John C. Stennis.

On the seventeenth of August 2004, I checked in on the ship. One department received all the Sailors who checked in and processed us for a period of two weeks until we were released to our mother division. This department took all new arrivals through orientation by teaching us all the ethics and good manners of the ship. We are also shown all the various departments of the ship in order to know your way around the boat. A carrier is a big ship of over five thousand Sailors who wake up every day to go about normal business.

It is not a joke at all to be on a nuclear carrier. The workload and movement of Sailors are rampant. We went through two weeks of orientation successfully and were released to our divisions. Within those two weeks, you only wake up and go to the classroom of the ship and wait for the various departmental heads or representatives to come and tell us of their expectations. We have two regular galleys namely forward and aft. The forward galley is used as speed line while aft is used as the main line galley. Food items such as burgers, French fries, hot dog, chili, etc are cooked and manned by the squadron cooks. The permanent cooks of the ship normally man the aft galley with main line items ranging from breakfast to mid-rat meals. Basically, on a carrier when we are on deployment, we the cooks are feeding the crew twenty-four hours and seven days in a week.

These two galleys prepare food all the time including grab-and go in the Mess Decks area. At the same time, there is a a pressure on us to prepare more food. When I think of the small ship in which I was before I came on a carrier, it is like a joke to complain about workload. When you see the feeding line during chow time, it is all the way down the hanger bay two. The crew works hard and when it is time to eat, they line up, wasting no second to eat. You may spend quite some time in line before getting closer to the Mess area to get food to eat.

Every department you have to go for a service on a carrier, you have to be in a line because of the large number of people. You are dealing with five thousand and over Sailors on a daily basis and life goes on like that. As soon as I checked into Food Service Division, I was put to work in the aft galley. I began working in the night shift. I go to work in the night and sleep during the daytime. At six p.m., you have to be at quarters for instruction and ready to enter the galley to assume night assignment.

The night shift on the carrier comes in to cook for mid-rat, clean the galley, put all the breakouts in coppers in order to thaw out and then begin to cook the breakfast. At four thirty a.m., we begin serving breakfast up to seven a.m. and then the line is closed. Right after we secured breakfast, then we quickly cleaned the galley and handed it over to the day crew who are already standing by to enter. There was no time to waste around. We get things done quickly, efficiently, and simultaneously. Our objectives are well-defined so as to put more urgency in the tasks set before us.

Few weeks after I got onboard the Stennis, the ship pulled into Sasebo in Japan for a port visit. It is one of the Navy's favorite port visits. Sasebo is one of the bases for the U.S. Navy as far as her Seven Fleet activities are concerned. Both Japanese Maritime Self Defense Forces and the U.S. Navy share the same port mutually. It is situated on the Northwest corner of the Island of Kyushu approximately one and a half hours from Fukuoka city.

USS John C. Stennis crew spent some days off hard work for fun in Sasebo. Earlier on, I had the chance of knowing Kadena Air Base in Okinawa Japan. It is very big base as compared to Sasebo. Okinawa is the largest island in the Ryukyu chain and is the base for U.S. and Japan under its Security Treaty. The base is the home for the U.S. Marines, some Sailors and their dependents. Under the Security Treaty between the U.S. and Japan, the base shall provide for mutual defense for Japan and ensures regional security.

We rocked it in the popular night club on the base of Sasebo. It was full of Sailors and civilians as well. The look in the face of the Sailors demonstrated that we really had fun and I personally felt everyone deserved it. We had a chance of visiting Ginza Arcade's shopping mall. It was also an opportunity to get to know Japanese culture and to experience their lifestyles. Although some of the locals protested against the nuclear carrier visit, the overall atmosphere was friendly and outstanding. The ship spent four days there and went back to sea. We left Sasebo on the twenty-fifth of August 2004.

I initially started my degree course when I arrived onboard the carrier. You can imagine a busy cook doing an online course on a carrier with five thousand and over Sailors. Getting internet access at sea was not easy at all. First of all, the internet service at sea is very slow. Also, we had less than an hour to stay on the computer and you have to get up to give the chance to another person to log on. There are a lot of shipmates standing by to log on.

You cannot just walk in and start using the computers in the ship's library. The rule was that you have to come and sign for it first ahead of time. I submitted some assignments to my school while we were in Sasebo, Japan. Time was not on my side at all to do my courses. I became annoyed and impatient. While typing assignment, all of sudden, I will receive a warning notice about the remaining time left. I had no choice than to wrap it up and log off. Such was the situation in which I was onboard the ship.

It came to a time when I started missing assignments because of heavy schedules and lack of internet access. I couldn't cope with the workload and the short time given to us in the library to use the internet. At the same time, I kept on pushing the assignments slowly until the ship pulled into Kuala Lumpur in Malaysia.

Malaysia is a beautiful country and has developed very fast. Stennis made the stopover on the first of September 2004 for four days port visit. We docked at Port Klang. The English language is well-spoken in Malaysia, so getting around was not a problem at all. As a Ghanaian onboard the ship, I was particular about the infrastructural development in that country as compared to my country. Both Ghana and Malaysia got Independence in 1957. While Ghana had Independence on 6th March 1957, Malaysia gained its Independence from the British on August 31st, 1957.

I admire the eighty-eight-story circular towers which are in the heart of the city shopping mall. Upon arrival, we boarded the contracted buses from the Port to downtown. Not long before, I realized that Malaysia has a mixture of Asian cultures. They are friendly and nice. There are a bunch of shopping malls as well as modern architecture. Their food is spicy, and I love it. The Ringgit is the Malaysian dollar. The currency code is abbreviated as MYR but widely known as RM. There are ATM machines everywhere and credit cards are accepted. The first thing I asked for while was on liberty was internet access so that I could submit my assignments. I found one and was happy to submit my assignments. I even used a credit card to pay for that transaction.

As I said earlier, I was watching the development in Malaysia closely to that of my country Ghana. I found out that both countries are all members of the Commonwealth of Nations. I am grateful to the U.S. Navy for giving me the opportunity to personally see the progress of that country. The capital and the seat of the Malaysian government is Kuala Lumpur and that is exactly where my ship made a four-day visit. A look from the people revealed a mixture of Chinese and Indians. The majority of the Malaysians are also Moslems. Stennis was cordially welcome, and we pretty much enjoyed our four-day visit. We got there on September first and left on the fifth of September 2004.

When we got underway from Malaysia, I could not get internet access any longer due to large number of Sailors onboard, workload, how slow the system became when the ship is far at sea. I had to withdraw from the Degree courses. I sent email to the school authority explaining the circumstances surrounding my job. I equally expressed my willingness to continue my course upon arrival with the ship from deployment.

We headed back to sea to conduct operations when the ship left Port Klang in Malaysia. The ship passed through Western Australia and we visited Perth/Freemantle. That was my second time visiting that place. We spent a few days and started heading toward home. On our way, we passed by Hawaii to pick up tiger cruise. Finally, Stennis returned from deployment to her homeport in San Diego on the first of November 2004.

Upon arrival, I reapplied to Colorado Technical University and luckily was granted permission to continue from where I left from. At the same time, the ship was getting ready to effect a home port change from San Diego to Kitsap in Bremerton, Washington. I stayed onboard from November 2004 until we moved to Bremerton. A lot of Sailors who learned about how it frequently rains in Washington State did not want to relocate from San Diego to this place.

Those Sailors who for some reasons did not want to come to Washington State with Stennis transferred to other ships and shore duties before the ship got underway to Bremerton. Since I have been stationed in Bremerton right from A School, I am used to the weather, so it did not bother me again. No wonder because of constant rainfall in Washington State, it is called the Evergreen State. I enjoyed few months with the ship in San Diego and could not wait to come back to my usual Northwest. The weather in California is pretty much sunny most of the time just like that of my country Ghana. Once you are relocating to Washington State, you should be ready for long-lasting winters whether you like it or not.

At long last, on the eighth of January 2005, the USS John C. Stennis eventually effected homeport change from North Island from San Diego to Bremerton Washington State in Kitsap Naval Base. It was emotional to those Sailors who wanted to remain in California. Unlike somebody like me who closed my apartment for some months just to be with the ship until that hour. I was very anxious to get back home since home sweet home. I could not wait to hear underway the ship goes knowing very well that we are just sailing to our new homeport.

The ship pulled into Delta pier since my previous ship Bridge -TAOE-10 used to be docked at this particular pier. Stennis came to replace USS Carl Vinson (CVN74) which earlier on left Bremerton for the last time for deployment and will return to her new homeport Norfolk in Virginia. Stennis moved to Bremerton in order to make use of the major overhaul facilities. It is also part of the Chief of Naval Operations to rotate the finest aircraft carriers from time to time so as to make it fair for the Sailors.

Before the Stennis even came back from deployment, the homeport change has been the topic under discussion on the ship. You can hear two or more shipmates discussing this issue on the boat. A few days before departing from San Diego, the ship loaded personal vehicles of Sailors and shipped other cars. The various representatives including the police department of Kitsap County, were onboard to provide the needed information to Sailors coming to Bremerton for the first time.

Those Sailors who have already relocated their family members to Bremerton were on the pier to welcome their loved ones. I was happy to come back home after I left in July 2004 to join the ship on deployment until it was time for homeport change. On the nineteenth of January 2005, the supposed elevens months Dry Dock Planned Incremental Availability started.

As soon as the ship landed in her new homeport in Bremerton, I was sent to Sea School at Olympic College. Once I completed the course, I reenlisted under STAR Program, and I was advanced to Second Class Petty Officer. I was encouraged to go to school in order to be promoted as a result of the tremendous effort I always put up into my assignments. The Navy therefore enrolled me in the Culinary Arts Department of Olympic College to study General Mess Operations Training (A-800-0030).

I Began the course on January 10th, 2005, and completed it on February 11th 2005. While I was on my previous ship, the USS Bridge AOE-10, I had a similar opportunity to sturdy at the same school Olympic College. That happened in 2002. It is good to take pride in getting your job done. Based on that, the Division sent me to pursue Private Mess Management Operations Training.

Upon completing the STAR Program, I was advanced from Culinary Specialist Petty Officer Third Class (CS3) to Culinary Specialist Petty Officer Second Class (CS2). As a Second Class, you are in pay grade E-5. Within the same year, the John C. Stennis was judged the Second Runner Up in the Captain Edwards Ney Award Program in Food Service. I benefitted from the effort we put in and was chosen with some colleagues to attend a course at First Coast Technical Institute—the School of Culinary Arts which is located in Saint Augustine in Florida.

While we were in the school, we had the chance to study Garge Manger Competencies, Baking and Pastry Arts. We also visited some Industries such as Seafood Processing Plant, San Sebastian Winery, St. Johns Food Service Distributors, ACF National Office, Chef Certification and last but not the least, Movsovitz & Sons Distributors. We had fun and a good time doing this course and were presented with Advanced Garde Manger/Pastry Arts Certificate on the nineteenth of August 2005.

Docking Planned Incremental Availability (DPIA) saw the ship removed from water and placed in the dry dock. Information from a reliable source revealed that this was the first time the Stennis was undergoing through that period since her commissioning into service. This idea is to maintain the material condition of the ship at a very high level so that she can last as has been the case.

A lot of civilian employees and contractors of PSNS and the crew worked hard in order to put the ship back to her regular shape. Painting and repairs were some of the jobs for the crew. The galleys went through a major rehabilitation. Waterline repair was given a priority and in December 2005, the ship was back to sea for trials.

The regular galley activities were relocated outside the ship temporarily to the Barge. All the food were offloaded. When the ship was ready to re-open cooking onboard, we had to clean the various galleys several times and certify them. Both the Mess Decks and the galleys were all given a new look during the dry dock period. I was personally impressed by the job they did.

My time onboard USS John C. Stennis eventually came to an end during the dry dock moment. I was getting all my paperwork done in order to go to shore duty. I initially got two choices. Either to make a choice between Nevada and the Bangor Military Prison known as the Brig. I finally got Bangor and was hoping to stay in the area. For some reasons, I could not make it there. The last choice I had was the Naval Air Station in Oak Harbor on Whidbey Island.

All these times, I still have been working on my degree. I can recollect how I have to submit a tuition assistance application to the Food Service Officer signing and for onward submission to Navy College Kitsap Bremerton Base. I have been to that office several times. They might be tired of me. Who knows? The bureaucracy was too long. I am very thankful to the Food Service Officer during the time I was onboard USS John C. Stennis.

Life on a carrier was quite challenging to me but overall, it was a good experience. Imagine how many cooks are on a carrier. I bet you there are a lot of Culinary Specialists on that type of ship. And in the middle of it all, I was recognized for the effort I put into my assignments. It is good to always let your light shine in wherever you go. It pays off in various ways without you personally taking notice of it. Your leadership is watching everyone in general. Just continue to do your good job. Don't say because your fellow worker is lazy so you must as well behave like that. You are not the same as that coworker.

Society is dynamic and we don't all come from one home. In every workplace you will meet different types of people. Some groups of people know the reason why they are there. Others don't just care about what is going on. There is a need to identify yourself and how one should behave.

It is like a classroom where you have three types of students namely average, below average, and above average.

My Naval career so far has given me the opportunity to learn about the differences in human nature. Born from a developing country, went to school over there with an accent and now making a living in the United States means a lot to me. I will never forget about my experiences. Some of them are good while others are really bad. However, all these obstacles will let you grow from strength to strength.

All said and done, my time onboard USS John C. Stennis was up, and I had to go on shore duty. I finally left the boat on twenty-fourth of January 2006. That morning, the ship was getting ready for underway. I had to hurry up, otherwise the brow was going to be secured and I could not come out. I was lucky I made it. I went on leave for thirty days. I am personally thankful to the Food Service Officer who was around at that time frame. He several times congratulated me on my token contribution in the Food Service Division.

I met a Storekeeper Chief Petty Officer from Nigeria who constantly encouraged me when the going was though. He left for shore duty in San Diego. He left me an unforgettable and an impressive memory. At the time I was checking onboard the ship, I was kind of scared and was not sure of lifestyles as well as workloads. I did not know exactly what a carrier looked like inside the ship. But as time went by, I was able to withstand the tough moments and everything that came with them. You would never know what your future has in store for you until then.

I want you to get prepared for any eventuality which can come across your path one day. It is always good to get prepared as it is often prevention is better than cure. I made so many friends on the USS John C. Stennis. When I was walking on the passageways, some people commended me on good work done in the galley, even though I don't recollect rendering them a service.

I met a friend who is from Liberia. He was a DK2. He was a nice guy and a gentleman. He helped me several times and I also reciprocated. Another hardworking guy I met on the ship came from Ghana. We became friends and he was popularly known as Edem. He worked at Security Department on the ship until he left the ship to shore duty. The two of us were in the club shaking it off on most cases while on liberty.

MY THIRD COMMAND

I left the ship for shore duty on the twenty-fourth of January 2006. I went on leave for thirty days and checked in to my new command on the twenty fourth of February 2006 at Naval Air Station in Oak Harbor, Whidbey Island. The fact that I came to Washington State in April tenth, 2001, I had never heard of Whidbey Island until I have to go there for three years on shore duty. Before my leave was over, I made sure I drove there ahead of time in order to get to know my way to the base.

I began driving from Bremerton up to Port Townsend to board the ferry. The ferry takes thirty to thirty-five minutes to cross from Port Townsend to Keystone. Within another half an hour drive, you are in Oak Harbor, Whidbey Island. I used two hours to make the journey from Bremerton to Oak Harbor. Initially, I will depart my house from Bremerton on Sunday afternoon for Oak Harbor and returned to Bremerton on Friday night.

Somewhere along the line, I became tired of long driving and all those up and down. I realized that you don't only have to drive under the influence of alcohol before getting into an accident. Fatigue is also an important factor which can lead an individual to get accident. One day, I just got fed up and moved from Bremerton to Oak Harbor and this was the place I started writing this book from.

The Island of Whidbey in Washington State is about eighty miles north of Seattle. It is roughly one and half hours away from the north of Seattle with a latitude of forty-seven degrees, twenty-one minutes north and a longitude 122 degrees, thirty-nine minutes west. It is believed to be the second longest island in the continental United States. History has it that Naval air Station Whidbey Island -NASWI was set up on September 21st in 1942 right at the time of World War II.

I never heard of this place before I received my orders for shore duty. It is a good place to raise kids at the time. It is calm with a few drinking bars for we Sailors and restaurants. Mi Pueblo was entertaining military personnel during the weekends and also on special celebrations. You have to drive outside if you really want to have fun in those days. Sometimes, I wondered how Oak Harbor town would have been without the presence of the military establishment in the area.

A dance club called Element was opened at the time I was there in Oak Harbor. That was the venue for we the Sailors to go and have fun during the weekend. It was a good place until I left. It was filled with gorgeous ladies across the borders of Vancouver in Canada. I thought I was going to see a harbor when I first came here but to my surprise, there was none. I was attached to the NAS galley on the base. We did our best to feed the Sailors on the base as often has been the case for Culinary Specialists. I was the STB Watch Captain—responsible for the presentation, preparation, and operation of a large ashore facility serving over 1,300 meals daily. I was also the supervisor of both the Mobile Canteen and the fast-moving line. It was very tedious and hard-working job but rewarding.

MY FOURTH COMMAND

I checked onboard USS Abraham Lincoln CVN 72 on March seventeenth 2009 in Everest in Washington. Abraham Lincoln is the fifth Nimitz-class aircraft carrier in the United States. The ship is said to be the second Navy ship to have been named after the former President Abraham Lincoln. The ship's home port was by then in Everest, Washington State.

This is about the Carrier. The ship is named after the 16th US President Abraham Lincoln of the state of Illinois. He was born on February 1809 near Hodgenville, Kentucky and lived there until the age of seven. At that time, his family moved to southwestern Indiana where they lived until 1830. During the sojourn in Indiana, Lincoln made a trip down the Mississippi to New Orleans, La., that probably provided his first face to face confrontation with slavery as an adult. In 1830, Lincoln moved to Illinois with his father's family but struck out on his own the following year.

Abraham Lincoln became the United States' 16th President in 1861, issuing the Emancipation Proclamation that declared forever free those slaves within the Confederacy in 1863. The USS Abraham Lincoln (CVN72) was launched on 13th February 1988 and subsequently commissioned with the US Navy on 11 November 1989. She was by then and still a member of the United States Pacific Fleet. The ship is administratively responsible to Commander, Naval Air Forces Pacific, and operationally served as the flagship of Carrier Strike Group Nine and host to Carrier Air Wing Two until 2012.

I initially worked in the galley for few days and then sent to Cargo (Storerooms). I spent six months working in Storerooms (JOD) and came back to the galley to become Watch Captain. On April 16, 2009, Lincoln started its planned incremental availability maintenance cycle at the Puget Sound Naval Shipyard (PSNS), Bremerton Washington State. I was a Watch Captain on the Barge in Bremerton until the ship went back to Everett.

The objective of the Planned Incremental Availability yard period is to refurbish Abraham Lincoln's shipboard system in order to meet the anticipated 50-year service life of the ship in addition to an upgraded Local Area Network system. Beginning 1st December 2009, the ship began daily flying squad, general quarters (GQ), and integrated training team (ITT) drills in preparation for its first underway period following its current maintenance cycle.

On 13th January 2010, the carrier completed upgrades and repair at Puget Sound Naval Shipyard. The carrier was to be assigned to carrier Strike Group Nine. On 3rd February 2011, the ship was awarded the Battle Effectiveness Award for its high standards of excellence and combat readiness. On 9th December 2010, the US Navy officially announced that Naval Station Everett in Washington State was the new homeport for the USS Nimitz (CVN-68), replacing Abraham Lincoln, which would be undergoing its scheduled Refueling and Complex Overhaul (RCOH) at the Northrop Grumman Shipbuilding, Newport News shipyard in Virginia which was scheduled to begin in 2013.

On a carrier, Food Service Division has a lot of storerooms. We have two big dry storerooms, a freezer, fruits and vegetable storeroom often referred to (FFV). These storerooms are very big and filled to capacity all the time and are located at the AFT side of the ship. We have other storerooms located at the FWD part of the ship. After being a Watch Captain at the AFT galley for a period of time, I was rotated to the Chief Petty Officers Mess popularly known as CPO Mess.

On 1st March 2011, the news media reported that the US Navy had awarded Northrop Shipbuilding at Newport News a huge sum option under a previously awarded contract to plan Abraham Lincoln's RCOH. Upon authorization, the ship's RCOH was anticipated to begin in 2013 and it was scheduled to take between three and four years to complete.

The US Navy announced that Abraham Lincoln will shift its homeport from Everett, Washington, to Newport News in Virginia for its Refueling and Complex Overhaul on 1st August 2012. We left Everett for the deployment that would take the ship around the world and eventually to Newport News in December 2011. On 7th August 2012, Abraham Lincoln arrived at Norfolk Naval Station following an eight-month deployment to the US Navy's 5th, 6th and 7th Fleet areas of responsibility, in preparation for her Refueling and Complex Overhaul at Newport News.

By mid-March in 2013, USS Abraham Lincoln had been towed over and docked at Newport News, and the RCOH work had begun. In 2012, I picked 1st Class and acted as Leading Petty Officer for Food Service Division. Early September 2013, I transferred to Shore Duty at Bangor Base Galley.

MY FIFTH COMMAND

I arrived to Bangor Naval Base Kitsap in Washington State on October third 2013 and was assigned as a Watch Captain after occupying the position of LPO on a carrier. I was in-charge of one of the watch rotations namely Port and Starboard duty days. I had three junior cooks known as CSs on Watch. We assumed the watch on Monday morning after Quarters—and work all day on Monday and Tuesday then we get off on Wednesday morning after Quarter. We then come back on Friday morning to assume the Watch after breakfast and work throughout the weekend up to Monday morning.

After working for a while as a Watch Captain, I earned my way to become Galley Supervisor. As a Galley Supervisor, I worked from Monday to Friday and was under training to stand Command Duty Officer popularly watch known as (CDO). The Galley Supervisor will oversee all kitchen operations such as food preparation, cooking, serving, and cleaning of equipment.

Galley Supervisor oversees food breakouts to the galley, putting it away, thawing, preparation under hygienic conditions, serving it to the crew, and cleanliness of galley spaces. The Galley Supervisor equally mentored and trained all the cooks on both Watches in daily preparation of breakfast, lunch, dinner, and ordering of food procedures from the Jack of the Dust referred as the Storeroom Custodians. Both Galley Supervisor and Watch Captains ensure proper cooking techniques as established by NAVSUP P-486, and NAVSUP P-7, often known as The Armed Forces Recipe Service.

As Culinary Specialists, we are committed to an inclusive and diverse workplace that values and supports the contributions of each of us with our Navy Core Values like Honor, Courage, and Commitments. We get the job done with unparalleled results. Part of my job is to lead the smooth execution of numerous special holiday and heritage meals which directly improved Sailors' morale.

As time went on, I climbed to the position of Leading Petty Officer's job (LPO). The Leading Petty Officer assignment in US Navy is very big one. The Leading Petty Officer (LPO) is a title usually given to a First-Class Petty Officer and you are the "go-to person" of the Division responsible for leading Sailors in the Division to accomplish their mission and assisting the Leading CS in accomplishing the various administrative tasks. Basically, the LPO will be responsible to the Leading Culinary Specialist for the good order and discipline of food service personnel, training, administrative duties, and for the care, operation and upkeep of all assigned equipment and spaces. You must have knowledge of how food service operates in general. All your Sailors will come to you with all their questions. Also, they have to pass through you before going to the higher chain of Command such as The Chief, Senior Chief, Master Chief and Food Service Officer. Luckily for me, I was LPO on USS Abraham Lincoln before checking in to Bangor Base, so it was easy for me.

While working as LPO, I changed my mind to cancel my shore duty and return to sea. I spent two years of three years shore duty and the detailer sent me to USS Kearsarge

LHD-3 in Norfolk Virginia. I was in Bangor base from October 3rd, 2013, up to January 15th, 2016. On February 18th 2016, I flew with some Sailors from TPU in Norfolk to join my new ship USS Kearsarge LHD-3 which was in deployment and made a stop-over in Bahrain.

MY SIXTH COMMAND

USS Kearsarge LHD-3 is a flagship for the Kearsarge Amphibious Ready Group (ARG), with the embarked 26TH Marine Expeditionary Unit (MEU). It is deployed in support of maritime security operations and theater security cooperation efforts in the U.S. 5TH Fleet area of operations.

Kearsage is the third ship of the Wasp-class multipurpose amphibious assault ships. The mission of the ship is to embark, deploy, land and support a Marine landing force. The ship was specifically designed to accommodate air cushion, landing craft (LCAC) for fast troop movement over the beach and AV-8B Harrier aircraft to provide close-in air support for the assault force. Kearsarge can also carry up to 26 Navy/USMC helicopters for troop movement, air support, and search-and rescue movements.

I joined the ship in deployment while it was in-port Bahrain. We spent some days there and went back to sea for business as usual. I was assigned to the galley as supervisor. It was my duty again to feed the crew with breakfast, lunch and dinner after which we cleaned the galley and got ready for night crew. I also supervised the breakouts coming from 5th deck to the galley through the conveyors for the night crew to prepare for the day crew coming in the morning.

I had a lot of rough days getting the food ready on time for the crew with all the evolutions going on. But I managed to prevail after completing a seven-month deployment to the U.S. 5th and 6th fleet areas of responsibility (AOR), May 3, 2016. The ship held a dinner reception on the flight deck aboard the ship while in Valencia, Spain for more than 100 Spanish distinguished visitors and 100 crew members also took advantage of the opportunity to participate in several community relation events to include participating in a 5K Walk/Run for Autism Awareness, and a visit to the Polytechnic University of Valencia where they were able to interact with the students and faculty.

Upon arrival to Norfolk, I visited my family back home in Ghana for a month. I returned from leave and to assume duty as Storeroom Custodian. We had twelve storerooms in Food Service Division on USS Kearsarge. We have one big freezer on fifth deck, followed by one FFV Storeroom and Chill Storeroom for eggs. Food Service also has one big Dry Storeroom. These Storerooms are linked to a Conveyor operated by the Engineering Department to assist Food Service receive Stores from the pier side to the Storerooms and the breakouts from the Storerooms all the way to the Galley.

On the Port side of the Mess Deck, all the way to fourth Deck, we have the Spice Storeroom, and Soda Storeroom. On the Third level, we can find Sauces and juices Storerooms. On the STB side of Mess Deck, we have milk, and Cereals Storerooms. Food Service receives Stores every two weeks in order to support twenty-one day cycles. Storeroom custodians provide their inputs to JOD supervisor and he or she in turn submit all food items in low limit to the Record Keeper to be put in FSM (Food Service Management System) which will be reviewed by Food Service Officer and onward approval and submission to Prime Vendors which will come to the ship in the forms of stores.

Receiving Stores for Food Service in the U.S. Navy is a big evolution. Stores are received both in-port and at Sea in underway which is known as Replenishment At Sea. Normally, the Navy Prime Vendors notify the Ship of the date the Food ordered will be arriving. This date is communicated to Supply Officer, and to the entire Supply Department and to Food Service Officer. As Storeroom Supervisor, we do two days breakouts to the Galley in order to re-arrange Storerooms and make a space.

Engineering Department is notified to ensure that the Conveyors are tested and ready to go. Duty Sections and Civilian Helpers known as Stevedores are contracted ready for Store receiving days. I understand that Stevedore operations were established by the United States Army to provide movement of supplies through ports in support of the American Expeditionary Forces during World War 1. Communication has been the key to planning a successful store load-out both in port and at sea. Food Service division and the rests of Supply Department can receive over three hundred pallets of foods and other supplies.

While the ship is docked in port Norfolk, Food trucks start arriving as early as 5:00 am through Security checkpoint to the pier side of the ship. We the Storeroom Custodians usually come to work as early as possible in order to set-up the rollers on the STB side of the Mess Deck all the way to the Conveyor. Engineering always sends one personnel to overall supervise the food loading operation from the Conveyor to the last desk where the Duty Section or the Stevedores line up to get the food to the various storerooms.

Food Service personnel are trained ahead of time by the Engineering Department to handle the Conveyor. There is always one Food Service Supervisor, one person to load the food to the conveyor and the safety personnel instant stopper. The safety personnel hand is all the time on the emergency stop button.

The day of receiving stores on USS Kearsarge is normally referred as Supply Department's stores evolution. It is not just Food Service Division. We have the Logistics Specialist (LS), and Ships Serviceman (SH) all sharing Hangar Bay all the way to Mess Deck. Logistics Specialist Sailors manage inventories of repair parts/general supplies and distribute mail for ships, squadrons, and shore-based activities.

They procure, receive, store and issue material and repair components. The Navy Ship Stores program provides quality of life goods and services, including barber and laundry services, basic sundries and other convenience store items, such as tobacco, vending machine products, and uniforms, at reasonable prices.

Receiving stores and getting all to the various storerooms normally takes two to three hours and even more than that. Delivery schedules are coordinated prior to arrival to ensure availability of equipment and personnel. The U.S. Army Veterinary Service is responsible for the Food Safety and Product Compliance Evaluations before Stores are brought on the ship in the first place. This is part of Military Medical Veterinary Inspection Responsibilities. Food items are inspected to ensure that the product being received is the item, type, style, and grade as ordered. Adequate storage space will be made available and working parties will be obtained.

When we manage to put the food in the various storerooms, then the next step is to re-arrange the food. Food items are stowed by date of manufacture or date of receipt in order to facilitate the breakouts of food to the galleys, inventories and proper rotation of stocks. Cases and boxes are stowed on grates and not be placed directly on the deck. The storeroom custodians have to ensure open spaces between stacks of cases and pallets in order to allow maximum ventilation. Lack of air circulation in the storerooms will damage your perishable food items.

Smoking in food storage areas is strictly prohibited to avoid fire and to prevent certain food items from absorbing the odor of smoke. Food items are stored in their original containers and wrappers as well. Food Service Officer normally inspect the various storerooms for signs of damage, spoilage, insect infestation, rodent contamination. When it is time to issue or do breakouts to the galleys, the oldest food supplies on hand are issued first. We referred to this process as "first in, first out" popularly known as (FIFO).

As storeroom custodians, the above processes described are our normal routines and you must get use to them when you are assigned to work in Cargo. Also, your storerooms are known as accountable spaces for Food Service Officer and as such, must always be locked. When forced entry or the storerooms are found not locked, this must be reported to the Food Service Officer so that the necessary actions will be taken to rectify this problem. The first thing done when storerooms are found not locked or a forced entry is detected is stock taking or inventory taking.

All storerooms will be counted to make sure that theft did not take place. This is done to painfully punish the storeroom custodians due to their own negligence for not making sure that storerooms are locked. Wall to Wall (counting of food) is done when there is incoming Food Service Officer to relieve the outgoing Food Service Officer. Wall to Wall is also done when storeroom custodian is relieved, and a new person takes over. Basically, the storeroom custodians referred to as the Jack of the Dust (JOD), work with Navy's current inventory management procedures for receipt, inventory, stowage, and issue of food to the various galleys onboard the ship.

I was in charge of JOD until the LPO made chief and I have to assume LPO position. While doing the job of LPO somewhere along the line, I was reassigned again to go back to fix the storerooms because they have been messed up when I left. I executed these two jobs (LPO/JOD) and the moment came for me to hand over LPO position to a new person. I then became Galley supervisor in S2 Division until the ship came back from deployment.

Few days after deployment, I was assigned to S5 Division (Wardroom) as Leading Petty Officer (LPO). My Wardroom crew was not all that bigger than S2 Division. Also, the ship was scheduled to go to the yard for repair works. The time finally came, and we transferred the Food Service Operations to the Barge. We did a lot of cleaning in order to get the Barge ready. It was not easy to move to the Barge, but we made it somehow. While preparing and serving the crew and the Officers on the Barge, my time onboard the ship finally came to an end. On the 4th of February 2020, I checked out and headed to Newport Naval Base in Rhode Island.

MY SEVENTH/
LAST COMMAND

I checked out on the 4th of February 2020 from USS Kearsarge LHD-3 and drove with my family from Norfolk all the way to North Kingstown Rhode Island. We started the journey around 9:00 am in the morning and arrived to North Kingstown around 11:30 pm in the night. I drove alone in the car while my family followed me in the other car. It took us over 14 hours from Norfolk in Virginia to arrive to North Kingstown in Rhode Island. We stopped over for gas and food twice and then continued the journey. There was no police check points nor barriers from one State to another. You will see the signpost stating that you are departing from one State and then entering into another State.

I checked out on the 4th of February from my old command and checked into my new command on the 25th of February 2020. A few weeks after I checked in, then COVID-19 outbreak spread across the entire State of Rhode Island. The Governor closed down the whole State and everyone has to wear mask. The Newport Naval Base was shut down, yet the Galley still had to feed Officers in training. Once again, I was put in JOD. As Bulk Storeroom Supervisor, I led three Cooks (Culinary Specialists) in requisitioning, receipt, storage, and issuing of 450 subsistence line items valued at $1.5M while maintaining 99% of inventory validity.

At the beginning of the global COVID-19 pandemic, I assisted in coordinating with our prime vendor by obtaining single-served food items suitable for carry-out meals. I also ensured we had adequate stock on hand in order to support over 95,000 meals for personnel who were kept in rooms for two weeks before they were allowed to come and eat in the galley. I equally trained over twenty-six of our Sailors in all facets of Food Service Operations.

After working in the storeroom for eleven months, I became the galley supervisor. I supervised twelve cooks and over twenty Civilian Food Service Attendants in the monthly preparation and production of 103,827 meals. My supervision and coordination of all facets of the food service operation resulted in our galley—Ney Hall receiving 9.5 out of 10 possible points and Five Star status during the fiscal year 2021 Food Service Accreditation Assessment.

Once you check into the Naval Base Newport in Rhode Island, you have to qualify within few months as the Command Duty Officer known as CDO. As a CDO, you will be handling complex events while supporting over 15,000 personnel across 50 tenant commands and over 160 occupied buildings. In the course of executing my job as Command Duty Officer, I got into accident one day on a snow day with the duty truck. I am grateful to God that I made it alive on base that faithful day. However, I got injured on my left shoulder in the course of the accident. I feel the pain everyday even though I have been to hospital numerous times. With the passing of time, my Naval Career came to an end as a First-Class Petty Officer (PO1).

I took the promotion examination to be selected as Chief of the United States Navy several times. I passed the exams on five occasions, but I was not selected to be a

Chief. Most of my friends became Chiefs and Senior Chiefs. The worst of all, some of my junior Sailors behind me even became Chiefs. I became ashamed of myself, but there was nothing I could do. On July 31st, 2022 I finally proceeded on terminal leave and that was my last day onboard after serving for 22 years in the United States Navy. Glory to God for his protection and blessings over my life while I was in the service.

PROBLEMS
CONFRONTING
AFRICA CONTINENT

As I indicated earlier on, the idea behind writing this book is to highlight how I and my siblings were brought up in the village in Togo on cocoa farm and how the opportunity came my way to come to the United States of America. While relaxing at home in America, I think a lot and I am compelled to discuss the problems that are confronting my motherland Africa within myself. It is like talking and debating with myself. I am convinced that there are many desperate youths out there like me who want an elevation in life, yet the means and opportunities are not there for them unlike the youths in developed countries. My continent has become a laughing-stock in the eyes of the Western world, and I am personally ashamed of it.

I keep on asking myself every day a series of questions without finding answers. Why is my motherland Africa being far behind the rest of the world? Since I came to America and watching TV, I don't normally see anything good on their television about Africa. Every image I see is negative and degrading. The question is why? What are the problems confronting us? We are described as the hungry people, continent full of conflicts, starvation, undernourished, malnourished, vulnerable, diseases, poorest continent on earth well done by advertisement from Oxfam, World Vision, UNICEF, Red Cross life aid and others on Africa.

Every image I see is negative, degrading and the question is why? What are the problems confronting us? What can we do to remedy them? Are we really helping ourselves? These are some of the questions in my mind as I go about my personal business every single day. For the sake of those who are ignorant and naïve about Africa because of the type of questions I get on daily basis, Africa is a Continent. The question is what is a continent? A Continent is one of several landmasses on earth surrounded by sea. In the whole world, if my memory can serve me well, there are seven Continents namely Asia, Africa, Antarctica, North America, South America, Europe, and Australia.

There are 54 countries on the African Continent as per the United Nations, and they are under one body known as African Union (A/U). Also, they are individual nations with geographical boarders put by the colonizers from Europe. Even though they are under Africa Union, the colonial boarders still exist among them. Each country has a different currency unlike the United States has dollar as common currency among all member states. Throughout my Naval career, I have been getting questions like "Is Africa a country?" Do you guys live on trees and how is the jungle life like? How are the giraffes, monkeys, and lions? I was amazed and surprised when my fellow shipmates asked me such questions.

In the beginning, I get irritated when someone asked me such questions, but somewhere along the line, it did not bother me any longer. I rather took the opportunity to educate them since they are ignorant about Africa even though solid internet service is at their fingertip to do research. Africa Union exists only on paper. We are yet to have free movement of personnel, goods, and services across one boarder to another country. For my friends in the U.S. Navy who did not know much about Africa, I want to educate you a little about Africa. You guys need to also read about slavery, and the Berlin Conference of 1884 up to 1885.

There was time when Africa experienced slave trade known as the Atlantic slave trade, or Euro-American slave trade. It involved the transportation by slave traders of various enslaved African people to the Western World. It has been estimated that over 12 million slaves were shipped out of Africa to supply labor to the New World. In the course of transporting the slaves to America and the Caribbean, several millions died along the way. It was referred to as one of the greatest migrations although it was a forced migration of humans ever in history. With reference to history, the remnants of this narrative can be found across the American South, in the Islands of Caribbean, and in the nations of South America.

The slave trade regularly used the triangular trade route and its middle passage and existed from the 16th to the 19th centuries. It is very significant to note that the vast majority of those who were enslaved and transported in the transatlantic slave trade were people from Central and West Africa that had been sold by other West Africans to Western European slave traders. Other slaves were also captured directly by the slave traders in coastal raids. The Europeans gathered and imprisoned the captured slaves at forts on the African coast and brought them to America and the Caribbean. To better understand the beginning of the slave trade in Africa, you have to travel to the Cape Coast of Ghana to visit the slave castles.

Cape Coast castle in Ghana was built in 1653 and in the beginning, it was a wooden building constructed for trade in rubber and gold by the Swedish African Company under the direction of Hendrik Carloff who was the King of Sweden. It was later rebuilt in stone and the surrounding area became the site of the European struggle for domination of the major seaports along the Atlantic coast of Africa and later most of the trade changed into human beings. Between 1482 and 1786, clusters of castles and forts were erected along 500-kilometer-long coastline of Ghana. At that time. Ghana was called the Gold Coast due to its vast quantities of gold, and the Castle served as fortified trading posts offering protection from other foreign settlers and threats from African people. It began as a trade lodge constructed by the Portuguese in 1555 on a part of the Gold Coast, which later became known as the Cape Coast. As mentioned earlier on, in 1653, following Sweden's conquest of the Cape Coast, the Swedish African Company constructed a permanent wooden fortress for trade in timber and gold. It was reported that a decade later, the fort was reconstructed in stone when the Danes seized power from the Swedish.

History further stated that the castle then passed through the hands of the Dutch and even a local Fetu chief at some point, before being conquered by the British in 1664. Cape Coast castle has been used over the years for the developing of slave trade, which came to a peak in the 18th century. And by 1700, the fort had been transformed into a castle and also served as the headquarters of the British colonial governor.

While visiting Cape Coast castle, make sure to carry a handkerchief along with you to wipe some tears. Cape Coast castle and other forts marked the beginning of the slaves' difficult journey during the era of the slave trade. The castles were the last memory slaves had of their homeland before being shipped off across the Atlantic, and never to return again. The castle was holding gold, ivory and other wares, then gradually imprisoned African slaves, who were reduced to yet another commodity. For those who did not make it to the new world, the castles were the last place they ever saw on land. Their last shreds of hope would wither away with every day of captivity in the castles.

We have Assin Manso Ancestral Slave River Park as one of the largest slave markets for gathering people to sell into slavery. This location served as the place where slaves had their last bath before being shipped out of Africa. Per history, captured Africans in the interior of the continent are marched to the castles after taken their last bath at Assin Manso river. The captured are shackled and made to walk over 300 miles from slave markets in the north. As a result, they are made to take their last bath once they arrived at the river and then headed to the dungeons in Cape Coast Castle. History further stated that "on the seaboard side of the coastal slave castle, was "the door of no return," a portal through which the slaves were lowered into boats, and then loaded like cargo onto big slaving ships further out at sea, never to set foot in their homeland again and with a final goodbye to the freedom they once knew."

The Scramble for Africa Conference was organized by Otto von Bismarck, the first Chancellor of Germany. The purpose of the conference was the formalization of the Scramble for Africa. It also contributed to ushering in a period of heightened colonial activity on Africa continent by European powers to eliminate completely most existing forms of African autonomy and self-governance at that time. The Berlin Conference about dividing Africa was also known as the "Congo Conference." The Scramble for Africa,— the Partition of Africa, or the Conquest of Africa, was the invasion, annexation, division, and colonization of most Africa by seven Western European powers during a short period known as New Imperialism (1881 and 1914).

Africa continent became food on dinner table for European nations to colonize. The first German Chancellor Otto von Bismark called together the major Western powers of the world to negotiate questions and end confusion over the control of Africa continent. History stated that the countries represented at the time included Austria-Hungary, Belgium, Italy, the Netherlands, Portugal, Russia, Spain, Sweden-Norway (unified from 1814-1905), Turkey, and the United States of America.

According to research, out of the fourteen nations who attended the meeting, France, Germany, Great Britain, and Portugal were the major players in the conference controlling most of colonial Africa at the time. In 1884, Portugal proposed a conference in which 14 European countries would meet in Berlin (Germany) regarding the division of Africa, without the presence of Africa. You can now understand how Africa became a food on a dinner table for European nations as guests to eat. History mentioned that during the Berlin conference the European colonial powers scrambled to gain the control over the interior of the continent. The conference lasted until February 26, 1885—a three-month period where colonial powers haggled over geometric boundaries in the interior of the continent, disregarding the cultural and linguistic boundaries already established by the native indigenous African population.

A case in point was the Belgian King Leopold II who succeeded his father to the Belgian throne in 1865 and reigned for 44 years until his death. That was the longest reign of any Belgian monarch. Leopold was the founder and sole owner of the Congo Free State, a private project undertaken on his own behalf as a personal union with Belgium. He used Henry Morton Stanley to help him lay claim to the Congo, the present-day Democratic Republic of the Congo. At the

Berlin Conference of 1884-1885, the colonial nations of Europe authorized his claim and committed the Congo Free State to him. Leopold ran the Congo by using the mercenary Force Publique for his personal gain.

He extracted a fortune from the territory, initially by the collection of ivory and, after a rise in the price of natural rubber in the 1890s, by forced labor from the native population to harvest and process rubber. It is worthy to mention that Leopold's administration of the Congo Free State was characterized by atrocities and systematic brutality, including torture, murder, and amputation of the hands of men, women, and children when the quota of rubber was not met. In 1890, George Washington Williams used the term "crimes against humanity" to describe the practices of Leopold's administration of the Congo Free State.

By 1900, a significant part of Africa had been colonized by mainly seven European powers such as Britain, France, Germany, Belgium, Spain, Portugal, and Italy. It is important to note that in nearly all African countries today, the language used in government and in media is the one imposed by the colonial power, even though most people speak their native African languages. The Scramble for Africa is also known as the partition of Africa, or the Conquest of Africa, was the invasion, annexation, division, and colonization of most Africa by Western European powers with only Ethiopia (Abyssinia) and Liberia remaining independent. Africa was therefore, partitioned without wars between European nations as food on dinner table.

There were several reasons why European powers set their sights on the African continent. The first reason was the search for riches (constant raw material supply) which happened to be abundant in Africa for European industrial revolution at the time European countries were flourishing in the technology. Another reason why European nations were interested in Africa was their desire for exploration because Africa as continent by then was misunderstood. Furthermore, there was competition between colonial powers to conquer greater amount of land as an indicator of superpower than the other.

Additional large motivator behind African colonization was to bring religion—the desire to spread Christianity to the indigenous Africans through their missionaries. The last reason for Western Powers to colonize Africa continent was imperialism. Christianity was therefore, one justification that European powers used to colonize and exploit Africa. It is worthy to note that through the spread of Christian doctrine, European nations such as Great Britain, France, and Netherlands sought to educate and reform African culture.

Imperialism is a state policy, practice or advocacy of extending a country's power and dominion, especially by direct territorial acquisition or by gaining political and economic control of other areas, often through employing hard power especially military force. There is this idea of racial or cultural superiority with imperialism. Many European nations thought that they were doing a favor to those living on the African continent by introducing to them the modern way of life even if it has to come at the cost of destroying African established indigenous cultures.

An Excerpt of Letter from King Leopold II of Belgium to Colonial Missionaries in 1883 said "Your knowledge of the gospel which we wrote will allow you to order the Negroes (Africans) in any way you want, and it will encourage them to love poverty. Convince the Negro that the poor are happier and will inherit the heaven, and its very difficult for the rich to enter the kingdom of God. You have to detach yourselves from them and make them disrespect everything which they revere as sacred and gives them courage to confront us. I make reference to their mystic (spiritually) system which is a threat to our conquest. You must do everything in your power to make it disappear. By all means the Negros (Africans) must be made Christian, by only this way will they let go of their rich Culture and everything they respect about themselves."

A Facebook posting written by a white woman who had some very strong opinions about Black people and their Christianity stated that "For black people to believe in the same God that allow them to be enslaved, shows their level of intelligence. We are living in the age of INFORMATION! We gave blacks Christianity because it made them better slaves. Even my great grandpa told my dad once those blacks accepting Christianity was the best thing that ever happened to white slavers. The fear of Hell and promise of everlasting life is what finally kept the slaves from rebelling and running away. Lol and now days black people are still praising the very imaginary white guy who allowed them to be enslaved in the first place. Shouting and dancing with their wigs falling off in church lol. I am no racist but we all must admit that black Christian women are some funny motherfuckers. The only whites who believe in Christianity are the descendants of poor whites from those days. The rich whites didn't believe in that crap because they knew what it was being used for. Control over slaves and poor whites."

There are numerous police check points and barriers within one country to another country making it difficult to facilitate free trade among neighboring countries. There are a wide range of constraints, distortions and abuses related to intra-Africa fragmentation. These barriers to regional trade fall most heavily disproportionately on women and the poor. Even though Africa has been described as the continent of starvation, illnesses, wars, poverty, illiteracy, poor health, inadequate educational systems, language remains a major barrier. You may have heard that most Africa countries speak English language, yet other nations speak French, or

Portuguese. As a result, much translation is needed to ensure that everyone gets the message being put across.

Someone has to translate or interpret conversations back and forth from French to English, Portuguese, and Arabic. All these come at no small cost to business across the borders of African nations. Although there are several factors impeding cross-border free trade among Africa countries, effective communication is a prerequisite for trade among nations. Also, do you know that there are 41 currencies that serve the African continent? So, when you intend to travel or do business in Africa, these currencies can pose you a real challenge or problem due to frequent fall of exchange rate. With the coming of Africa Union, we need one single African currency.

With the establishment of African Union on July 9, 2002, in Durban, South Africa, AU has a continental body of 55 member states that make up the countries of the African Continent. AU was launched in 2002 as a successor to the formal Organization of African Unity known as OAU, of 1963-1999). Even though we have AU, each country is still an individual nation. African Union basically, exists on paper and still not practical. When exactly, no one knows. It is moving at a slow pace. Because there isn't a United Africa yet practically, we don't have free movement of goods, services, and personnel across the borders as indicated in earlier in this chapter. Each country has different currency, unlike the United States where we have a solid dollar is used all over its states.

The continent suffering from colonial rule and its impacts are still affecting Africa. The European countries entered into Africa under the false pretense of bringing Christianity and modern civilization into Africa. They asked African to close their eyes to pray, When Africans opened their eyes, the Westerners established a system of governance by exploiting, torturing and eventually conquered them. All the Africans had been taken from them to Europe to enrich their respective countries.

How will you feel to be a slave under torture in your own country, yet you could not do anything to remedy yourself? A lot of human resources were lost as a result of slave trade. The impact is still affecting Africa. Imagine how human beings were transported as commodities across the red sea, to India Ocean, not forgetting the Sahara route and the Atlantic Ocean. Some people argued out that slavery moment has passed so we should get over it. It is true that it has been abolished some years ago, but many problems facing Africa today are directly linked to the slave trade and colonization. No doubt about it.

The same European nations who rigged African countries from their natural resources are now turning around and claiming to be lending money taken from Africa to selfish old leaders of Africa-Aids. The next minute, we owe money to the same people who have taken our resources away to enrich their Western countries. I hear of African debt cancellation!! Instead of saying whatever I have taken away from you, I am returning it to you, the language rather is reframed differently. It is very pathetic, annoying and devastating.

Having said what happened to Africa during slavery, and to colonialism, let us take a look at what is going on now when we claimed that we are independent. The colonial masters are no more ruling us for years so things should be well with us, right? Don't you think so? Are they? I don't think so. Instead, there is more chaos. You will see child labor all over African continent. Children who are supposed to be in school learning are all hovering around the streets for survival. Their government officials turn their blind eyes pretending not to see them when driving to their various offices every day. You will see poverty, wars, corruption, hunger, starvation, malnutrition, prostitution, unemployment, political instability or frequent coups d'états as normal routines. Also, there is rigging of election where the winner is denied, while the looser uses all back door deals to be declared as the winner in order to continue to rule. All these problems have a direct impact on the children and the youths of Africa.

We should be concerned about educating our children and finding jobs opportunities for the youths but that seem to be forgotten by the government officials once they are voted into office. Children are forced to work under horrendous and unfavorable conditions. Young females are being forced to enter into early sexual acts against their will but have no choice to indulge themselves in such acts. These are countries that claimed to have leaders yet have turn their eyes away from the very problems they campaigned to solve. Human trafficking and other abuses of innocent children which have become rampant now must be denounced immediately.

In most rural areas in Africa, a large number of towns, and villages don't even have classrooms. Teachers have to teach under a tree or in dilapidated classrooms, but their government officials are flying in private jets. The money to fly a private jet can build classrooms across the nations. These are the very individuals who go to church on Sundays to pray to God to bless them and their countries. We have lower education rates which directly contribute to higher incidences of childhood marriage, teen pregnancy, HIV/ AIDS infection rates, and continued poverty among women and girls. For village and cottage students, daily commutes to and from schools is very long, challenging, and even unsafe.

If your country's educational system is free but no expansion on the facilities of the schools, you are going to have high enrolment rate, but low-quality outputs. You must have money to buy textbooks, and teaching aids for teachers to utilize. Schools with boarding facilities should be expanded and renovated. Money should be allocated to feed the boarders. Otherwise, there will be issues and a gender disparity at a certain stage resulting to poorer educational outcomes. All these factors mentioned above will result to a certain percent of school drop out with females in greater numbers.

Africa countries need to build more modern schools to address inadequate classroom blocks for students. There is inadequate supply of teachers in the rural areas due to dilapidated classrooms. Teachers posted in such places don't accept posting, while others vacate their post and return to the city. Low wages of salaries of teachers have been a major factor facing Africa countries' educational system. Politicians become rich yet cannot pay the teachers well, let alone increase their salaries. In the middle of educational problems in Africa, politicians' kids receive their education in America, and Great Britain.

Most African nations are suffering from poor road construction, potholes, leading to cars crashes, road accidents and numerous deaths every year. The bad nature of roads, such as dusty, and muddy are affecting citizens health resulting to respiratory diseases. Farmers and traders find it difficult to transport their produce to adjoining villages for sale as a result of the deplorable nature of the roads linking one town, or community to another. With these bad roads, government officials somehow can manage to drive on them to go and campaign for votes.

Most of the hospitals in Africa are suffering from lack of beds to the extent that some health care facilities are forced to suspend referrals from other hospitals due to congestion. Some patients sleep on the floors, while others are treated in plastic chairs, wheelchairs and even on the ground. Aside the lack of beds, one can site numerous abandoned health facilities, medical costs, lack of medicines and systemic corruption. As a result of the issue of brain drain of medical professionals, some doctors normally go outside Africa to practice elsewhere. You will assume that politicians will build more hospitals to ease the pressure on the dilapidated ones. No, they don't and rather, seek medical treatment in USA, Dubai, Britain and in Singapore.

In many African countries, the infrastructure is largely poor, talent and plans seem to be scarce for politicians. Poverty, famine, and disease affect a lot of countries. Open-air markets are an integral part of African societies. While some of them operate every day, others are on a regular cycle. When you are lucky to travel to Western nations from Africa, you can just picture how some parts of the world have so much and how Africa continent seems to have virtually nothing. It hurts me deep down my soul, but our politicians don't care about us. When fifty-four countries put their resources together in Africa, you can imagine how formidable the continent will become to confront its problems.

That reminds me of the dreams of the first President of Ghana in the person of Dr. Kwame Nkrumah. He was the pivot behind the movement for Independence of Ghana under British rule by then. He fought for Independent and by dint of hard work, Ghana became Independent on 6th March 1957. He stated that "The Independence of Ghana is meaningless unless it is linked up to the total liberation of Africa." What happened to his dreams for Africa? He cited the good example of the United States of America, and that of Soviet Union. We now have European Union, and the question is when will African Union be running?

Africa continent has a vast land for agriculture and can even feed the world yet, remains a net importer of food although it has 60% of the world's uncultivated arable lands.

There is hunger and starvation, and we are the same continent with the absolute number of undernourished people—have increased over the past 30 years. Africa has the land, the water is in abundance, the continent should be the one with greater potential to produce and export its excess products outside to the Western World, right?

The story is rather the other way round. With sufficient agricultural land to farm, there is poverty. Many farmers can only farm on small scale subsistence level. Peasant farmers lack education and as a result, the knowledge and skills are not available. They don't have resources to buy modern farming tools. Can the government do something about it? Of course, yes! Rewarding the hard-working farmer will be a morale booster. Subsidizing agricultural inputs would be of a greater help to agricultural sector. For agriculture to constitute the backbone of the economy of a country, the government has to play a major role. Organizing constant seminars to upgrade local farmers is very paramount. Subsiding fertilizer price will definitely help the farmers.

Poor rural people lack certain basic needs such as food, clothing, shelter, portable water. They have more mouths to feed and bills to pay, yet most of them are not employed. There is total lack of Sanitation, health care, pollution, and environmental conscience. Africa is going through such adversities. What should we do? Once again, it will require the various bodies of government to exhibit high level institutional integrity.

A growing continent suffering from the devastation of civil wars is ultimately in trouble. Hungry politicians come into power just to loot state coffers into private coffers and private foreign accounts. Instead of sticking to their campaign promises, they want to become rich quickly, thereby plunging the developing countries into more financial problems. African leaders have failed to build their various communities that can invest in the material well-being of the citizens. They have also failed to protect political, civil, and other rights, promote accountability, transparency, and the rule of law. Every citizen of Africa continent is law abiding in the western countries and in the United States. But in Africa, some leaders don't enforce the laws, so citizens behave anyhow. Maybe that is why there is total lack of sanitation and environmental consciousness in some nations.

They have also failed to ensure judicial independence, and the holding of free and fair elections. Some leaders are not ready to promote ethnic pluralism, tolerance, mutual respect, and peaceful co-existence among all the various tribes in their respective country. Africa continent is equally experiencing corrupt and autocratic leaders who are using state power as the yardstick to accumulate their country's wealth into private foreign accounts. They are using every illegal means, including bribery and corruption, extortion, and theft of public funds for their families and friends.

Wars are not the answer for developing countries, but somehow the post-colonial leaders of Africa are indulging in it with the help of Western nations who are financing warring factions for the sheer interests. Religion and ethnicity should not be a problem confronting Africa continent. The end result of wars in elsewhere is destruction of property. The very continent which suffered from slavery to colonialism should not be engaging in war of any kind. The least we have been left by colonial masters are now being destroyed by selfish politicians who don't have the interests of their countries at heart.

African countries should embrace ethnicity and religion as diversity of culture. Discrimination among ourselves will not help us. Politicians must ensure fair distributions of national cake. They should tackle unemployment problems for their youths. The end result of conflicts is always disastrous!! Always think about agricultural land, social amenities, the environment pollution, education, health care, roads, hospitals!!!! Think about the number of people who become refugees after wars. In one hand, African countries go to IMF/World Bank to borrow money for development. On the other hand, conflicts among tribes destroy all that we have borrowed to build. You can imagine how stupid we have become!!! Money borrowed is a debt and must be paid with higher interest rates or Western capture when we default from paying the debts. No wonder today, we have the system called neo-colonialism replacing colonialism. According to Dr. Kwame Nkrumah, "The essence of neo-colonialism is that the State which is subject to it is, in theory, independent and has all the outward trappings of international sovereignty. In reality its economic system and thus its political policy is directed from outside."

Somewhere I read that "If the owners of natural resources go around begging, then you should know there's something wrong with their minds." And that is the reality on the ground in Africa Continent. The Africa we have today is the one where government and their relatives are looting the country. Somewhere I read as well that "African educational systems have surprising outcomes. The smartest students pass with first class and get admissions to medical and engineering schools. The second-class students get MBAs and LLBs to manage the first-class students. The third-class students enter politics and rule both the first and second-class students. The failures enter the underworld of crime and control the politicians and businesses. And best of all those who didn't attend school become prophets and everyone follow them"

That is Africa for us now, it is very shameful. Another fact about some leaders in Africa is that "A bad system doesn't appear wrong to those who benefit from it. They do everything to defend it to the detriment of larger society."

Such leaders are using religion to back their wrong doings. It is very pathetic. Somewhere I read that "Religion does three things effectively: divides people, controls people and deludes people." This is where we have landed to in Africa now.

Politicians come to power on the back of mouth-watering promises to make life easier for their citizens. They promise a lot of rapid developmental projects with sod cutting but turn around to squander the money allocated for the same projects. We need to progress and not to go backward. Bribery and Corruption have been the main cause of frequent coups that disrupted African nations in the past. Nothing has change but rather got worsen. It might interest you to know that corruption occurs in both private and public sectors in African countries. Corruption can be seen in public procurement, the judiciary, police, public services, tax collection agencies, and custom administration to just mention a few. Money lost through corruption can be used to improve the infrastructural and transport network, education, healthcare systems, portable water, housing, electricity, and communication.

Corruption which is "dishonest, illegal, or immoral behavior" has become the quickest way of getting rich in African societies. The genuine and accepted ways to earn a livelihood are too slow for the majority of people. So, bribery which is "dishonestly giving money to someone in order to persuade them to do something in the form of help" has become the new order of the day in African nations. What do we see African politicians do when they are about to get a political power? They campaign with sweet words and convincing slogans. Everything they say is assumed in the name of development oriented. Their words convince the poor voter and the masses to give them the mandate. Once the politicians ascend to the presidency, that is it. They will start diverting money meant for national development into private foreign accounts.

The leaders then start appointing non-qualifying friends and family members (nepotism) in order to carry out their own political agenda. You will then start experiencing the abuse of public power for personal gains to the detriment of national interests. This is what is destroying the African continent. You have to call a spade exactly a spade. Government officials who are supposed to pay allegiance to the constitution of their country rather turn around to be in bed with the President of their country. You now have the President; judiciary and the legislation body all conspire to loot state coffers.

National interests gradually give away to selfish interests. Chasing easy money in order to live in luxury is no more identified as something that is morally wrong. Life become the survival of the giants over the poor middle-class citizens. Remember that these are the same politicians with fantastic ideas in opposition. Somewhere I read that "we are sitting on money, yet we are hungry." When your infrastructure is largely poor, yet you can afford to rent a private jet that causes 14K pound an hour at the expense of tax-burned poor citizens, then that particular African Country is gone.

Deliberate embezzlement of state money in the form of awarding projects so that the government officials can pocket some percentage of such project funds to the execution of shoddy projects are some examples worth mentioning. To get a job, you must pay money and if you are a female seeking a job, you must be ready to sleep with both government officials and private business managers. Some unqualified students pay money in order to be admitted. A policeman takes bribes to let small fish go scot-free. It is evidently clear that corruption occurs often in locally funded contracts, and companies are subjects to bribes when operating in rural areas.

When businesses are being asked for cola or favors from government officials in return for facilitating business transactions, we have red flags!!! Government officials using their positions to enrich themselves, that is willful exploitation of public office. That lead to "citizens in poverty, joblessness, in their broken homes and with shattered dreams." When a taxpayer's money meant for development is diverted for personal gain, it is the national economy which will suffer.

Government officials and politicians pocketing state money into Swiss accounts and elsewhere has become the order of the day. Such money embezzled is supposed to be allocated for building schools, roads, hospitals, potable water, investing into the agricultural sectors etc... All these neglects affect the poor rural folks. Who is to be blamed now that the colonial masters are gone, and our own African leaders are in charge of political affairs? It is we the Africans!!! We are the causes of the downfall of our own continent to a greater extent.

Superpowers have been calling Africa leaders' summit and the leaders of Africa have been parading and attending. We have had Forum on U.S.-Africa Leaders' Summit, China-Africa Cooperation Summit, UK-Africa Investment Summit, Russia-Africa Summit, India-Africa Forum Summit, France Africa Summit, Turkey Africa Partnership Summit, and Middle East and Africa Summit in the past. All these leaders in Africa are happy to be invited to receive financial commitments for infrastructure yet nothing is done after the funds have been received. They gather around themes to develop tighter and increase the welfare of their people together. They claimed to attach great importance to infrastructure development and agriculture and promote resilient health systems for their people but only few countries actually deliver on such electoral promises.

Parading the corridors of the colonial masters looking for aid is not the answer. Seeking for foreign loans to finance capital intensive projects that are of no use is just adding to foreign debts. Africa youths suffer while funds borrowed are diverted, instead of creating job avenues. These are some of the reasons why the youths of the continent are running away to seek greener pastures in the western world. In the course of doing so, some youth put their precious lives at risks.

Somewhere I read that "Of the 2021 total, 1,924 people were reported to have died or gone missing on the Central and Western Mediterranean routes, while an additional 1,153 perished or went missing on the Northwest African maritime route to the Canary Islands, according to UNHCR's newly report: Protection, saving lives, & solutions for refugees in dangerous Journeys." UNHCR report further stated that "Most of the sea crossings took place in packed, unseaworthy, inflatable boats-many of which capsized or were deflated leading to the loss of life." All these Africa youths losing their lives, yet their leaders are quiet. No actions are taken!! You will wonder what issues the Africa Union discusses when they meet in Ethiopia!!

Reading Desperate Journeys Refugees and Migrants Arriving in Europe and at Europe's Borders (January-December 2018), the report emphasized that "The number of refugees and migrants making the Mediterranean Sea crossing fell in 2018 but it is likely that reductions to search and rescue capacity coupled with an uncoordinated and unpredictable response to disembarkation led to an increased death rate as people continued to flee their countries due to conflict, human rights violations, persecution, and poverty."

No matter how we attribute part of poverty issues of the Africa continent to slavery and colonialism, we must also be prepared to hold our black leaders accountable for their lack of leadership styles. It is about that time they wake up from their slumber and live up to the expectations of their people. To me personally, if you don't have the interests of your people at heart and squandering the country's resources between friends and family, the military should take you out. You don't deserve to continue to serve as a President of that country anymore. Nelson Mandela once said" When you see that the government and their relatives are looting the country, you have to disobey, rise up, get on the streets, drive them out of the country, send them into exile and nationalize their illegal gains."

Imagine the numerous natural resources African countries have yet, are parading the corridors of western nations for free money to develop their countries. Some countries have gold, diamonds, manganese, bauxite, clays, kaolin, mica, columbite-tantalite, feldspar, chrome, silica, sand, quartz, salt etc... Other resources are cocoa, coffee, and oil. All these resources belong to just one country in Africa, but the President and his family and friends' government of that country are squandering all the funds. Other revenues and loans received all cannot be accounted for. The worst of all, there is not even a single school, nor hospital constructed. If you complain, you become the enemy of the government machinery. The foot soldiers of the governments in power will be sent to discipline you.

Somewhere I came across that "Government don't want an intelligent population because people who can think critically can't be ruled. They want a public just smart enough to pay taxes and dumb enough to keep voting and electing corrupt politicians."

Africa leaders brag of a land of knowledgeable people yet, you cannot see them as the right leader for their country. It is rather unfortunate that the people in leadership have no clue as to how to govern a country. Despite all the resources, the continent is still ranked bottom in the eyes of the western world. How long shall we continue to borrow or look for foreign aids which will even end up in the pocket of the greedy politicians? When will African union be functional in reality with all their resources together to benefit African citizens?

Somewhere I read "What is the difference between an Ordinary Thief (OT) and Political Thief (PT)? The ordinary thief steals your money, bag, watch, gold chain etc…but the Political Thief steals your future, career, education, health and business!! The hilarious part is: The Ordinary Thief will choose whom to rob. But you yourself choose the Political Thief to rob you. The most ironic one: Police will chase and nab the Ordinary Thief. But Police will look after and protect the Political Thief! That's the travesty cum irony of our current society! And we blindly say we are not blind!!! The stupid part of the whole issue is that we insult and fight the Ordinary Thief, but we fight each other for The Political Thief. The Ordinary Thief is referred to as "Hoodlum" whereas the "Political Thief is referred to as "Honorable." These are the scenarios we find ourselves in Africa.

It is time to advocate for a practical Africa Union right now!! The end result of wars, rigging of elections, hunger, starvation, bribery and corruption affect the innocent African children, the youths, women and elderly people in every society. These folks have nothing to do with the mismanagement of the resources of various Africa nations. With Africa continental government in place, all our raw materials will be processed in Africa member states and no longer in the well-orchestrated western nations. How can you have mineral resources in Africa, yet the processing industries are in Europe with finished goods sold back in double fold to

Africa? This is sickening and mind blowing with no common sense.

When you hear of frequent coups or political instability in Africa, don't be surprised. The Western countries are deeply involved because of their sheer interests. During turbulent period of African fighting to liberate themselves from European colonization, France for instance would repeatedly use many foreign legionnaire to carry out coups against elected presidents of those countries which were colonized. Remember that "without Africa, France will slide down into the rank of a third world power." Africa also deserves an atmosphere that is free and peaceful to conduct business without western influence. Africa governments in power should not go back to conduct colonial business at the expense of their people. They should ensure a peaceful atmosphere for the private sector to operate. We need to continue to invest on world-class infrastructure, housing units, building modern schools with modern teaching aids, hospitals to the remote areas of our countries.

Potable water should be provided in modern housing units to avoid the spread of diseases. We have not done fifty percent yet, but the funds meant for such developments are diverted to private accounts. We have not built factories and industries, but we have numerous churches and building national cathedral with government funds. Somewhere I read that "You have a serious problem if you don't see anything wrong with a society having 1 hospital, 2 schools, zero factory, and 165 churches."

Someone tweeted "In Ghana there are more churches than schools and hospitals put together; more pastors than teachers; more prayer camps than research centers; more drinking bars than manufacturing companies; and above all more talkers than thinkers. What kind of progress do we want?" A developed nation has finished building schools, roads, housing, markets, hospitals, extended electricity to every part of their countries. Potable water and hot shower are available to middle class-citizens including toilets in every household. There is stable internet, and thousands of TV channels to watch.

All governments systems all working perfectly 24/7. Emergency systems such as ambulances, firefighting and 911 are all in place. As a matter of fact, if you dial 911, ambulance, fire service, and the police will all assemble in short time to respond to your need. Africa leaders cannot ensure these basic humans right for their citizens with all the mineral resources nature has put at our disposal. What are we doing with our mineral resources!!

We need money to solve these basic needs, yet some presidents can afford to spend millions of dollars or euros on luxury-chartered jet at the expense of taxpayers. Some presidents are not thinking of building factories and industries that can solve unemployment problems for their youths. Somewhere I read that "Colgate (made in USA), Aqua Fresh (made in Britain), Close Up (made in England), Mentadent (made in Canada), Oral-B (Made in USA), and Sensodyne (made in Japan). Rich Prophets, Pastors and Bishops (made in Africa). We produce toothpaste, you produce anointing oil and prayers." What an insult for Africa continent!!!

XI Jinping President of China once said "The only thing the black man has inherited from Arab and European colonization is the religion that he practices and that's exactly what the colonizers wanted. Notice that in black countries, the Education is a disaster, the administration is corrupt, health is deplorable, but Religion is doing wonderfully well. Black people Rebels against everything except Religion. They even think they are more religious than those who brought them these concepts and that the colonizers are not good Christians. Black people even claimed themselves to be the original race of which Jesus Christ has descended. This is how far black people stupidity can go. Notice that any society that is full of superstitions, religious indoctrination, lack education and nationalism, is always ridden with violence."

Africa democracy is gradually declining as a result of some heads of state have moved to undermine term limits and even rigging elections to remain in power. Some Africa countries have dictators in a democratic clothing. What is the purpose of spending money meant for development projects to organize election and aftermath for the candidate who has not won to be declared the winner? Why can't we welcome democracy properly as it is done in the spirit of sportsmanship? Of course, in the context of two or more people, it is a fact that one person would eventually become the winner. Why can't the losing candidate accept defeat peacefully? The leaders are the same people knocking at the doors of western nations to negotiate for foreign aids in order to organize for free and fair elections. The real winner who represents the voice of the people is rather denied and declared the loser in full view of everyone. What is wrong with African leaders?

Rigging election results would not bring peaceful and harmonious atmosphere for normal business to be conducted. It adds to the plights of the country's population of poor, unemployed, and disenfranchised youth. You have a situation where a dozen people suffered gunshot injuries in clashes between political party supporters and a group of alleged security operatives. The hungry politicians don't have the interests of their people at heart. For people to die in an election so that you can be elected as a president is shameful. We have a lot of homework to do in order to redeem the name of our continent.

Another severe issue affecting African continent is unemployment. It is very sad and heartbreaking to a large number of graduates and other qualified youths who are ready and willing to work yet cannot find a job. Government in opposition had several plans to create jobs for the youth when they are voted in power. But once they are in power, they have no clues as to how to create jobs with all the revenues, mineral resources, and loans at their disposal.

Somewhere I read that "Ghana's youth employment challenge is vast and requires an all-round, deliberate, and consistent response." It stated that "youth unemployment and joblessness together constitute a major socio-economic and political problem in Ghana in particular." Unemployment is leading to high volume of rural and urban migration. Everyone wants to seek for a better lifestyle and work in the cities. They arrive to realize that they cannot get jobs. Nobody cares for anyone in the city but oneself. Because the youth cannot withstand the hardships of unemployment, they have no choice to indulge in petty crimes like theft, armed robbery, and prostitution.

It is interesting to know that in some countries in Africa, there is sex for job going on. It is a situation where a prospective employee or candidate for a vacant position is requested by the employer or the person in charge of recruitment to have sexual intercourse with him before being considered for the position whether they are qualified or not. This dirty behavior and many more are happening live in African countries like Ghana. It is about time we start reviewing our economic policies. How can a nine-year old girl on her way to school get raped? Now police finally arrested her attacker who even infested her with HIV just to release him because the guy paid bribe to them. Are we serious!!!

Other people have paid different forms of bribe to the police and the courts in order to escape punishments. You also have to pay to get a basic access to services that you are entitled to. The political thief with the political power enjoys a lavish lifestyle at the expense of the taxpayers. African people are daily being deprived of their basic needs such as clean water, food, health care, education, affordable housing, sanitation. According to a US state department report on Ghana "While the Constitution and law provide for an independent judiciary, the judiciary was subject to unlawful influence and corruption. Judicial officials reportedly accepted bribes to expedite or postpone cases, loose records, or issue favorable rulings for the payer of the bribe."

The report also stated that "A judicial complaints unit within the Ministry of Justice headed by a retired Supreme Court Justice addressed complaints from the public, such as unfair treatment by a court or judge, unlawful arrest or detention, missing trials dockets, delayed trials, and rendering of judgements, and bribery of judges." These are the plights of African people at the mercy of their politician thieves.

What is holding free trade across the borders among African countries? The leaders of Africa are parading the corridors of developed nations who are benefiting from free trade. African leaders are fighting over sovereignty of individual country and closing borders to their neighboring countries. Parents cannot provide three square meals for their households. Kids have to eat, wear clothes, shelter to rest after work, money to pay school fees, and the medical bills. Now we have a lot of broken homes because parents cannot control their children due to poverty. Imagine kids are hungry for food, and you the father or mother don't have money to feed them. They will not listen to you, and they will begin to grow without any morale value to impact their lives positively. How can you instill a sense of self disciple in the hungry and angry youth who will become future leaders?

All the above issues discussed are affecting the youth, and middle class and must be addressed urgently so that Africans can also begin to enjoy the fruits of their labors on earth, not to die and go to heaven before to enjoy it. Somewhere I read that "Your knowledge of the gospel will allow you to find texts ordering and encouraging your followers (blacks) to love poverty, like "Happier are the poor because they will inherit the heaven" and, "It's very difficult for the rich to enter the kingdom of God."

The continent needs a stable atmosphere to conduct everyday business and above all peace. Civil wars will not help us in any way or forms. In fact, it will only worsen the existing problems of Africa. Both human resources and properties have been lost through careless and selfish wars in the past in Africa. We need to continue to create greater awareness about HIV/AIDS. The only way we can alleviate this deadly disease is through sex education. The use of condoms should be encouraged. The best solution is abstinence and getting tested to know one's status.

African leaders must ensure equal educational opportunities for both boys and girls. The place for a woman as it has been the case in the past is no longer the indigenous kitchen in African mind. Women can perform marvelously as a man, given the same training and tools since we are in the era of modernization and technology. Africa must educate both boys and girls equally so that they can all face the challenges of the future. No more discrimination against women when it becomes to decision making within African indigenous societies. Parents choosing to send their male kids to school with the notion that the females cannot perform up to the same standard of the males is a baseless argument. Equality in every sphere of life is very important if African parents are to realize the full potentials of their children. Life skills are valuable lessons kids will use throughout their lifetime.

Decision making, health and hygiene, time management, cleaning, knowing how to do laundry, getting dressed and ready, and meal preparation should be taught to kids at home before heading to school. Africa governments must ensure that discrimination toward women in any form do not exist.

It is imperative to note that education is the only key to attaining higher intellectual abilities, status, management, and other decision making. Greater gender awareness can transform the prevailing distribution in careers and in other professions still regarded as more suitable for either men or women. Consider women as the ones for bringing up families and so they must be educated equally as men. Men prefer educated wives since they are in a better position to manage the income of their husbands more economically than uneducated ones. I urge our African parents as the first line of teachers, to endeavor their best in educating both genders equally.

One of the problems Africa Continent is facing is that Africa has become dumping ground of unwanted goods and commodities of the western world. It is estimated that about 15 million used garments for instance, pour into Accra every week from UK, Europe, North America and Australia, flooding the city's sprawling clothing market. Research further mentioned that an estimated 40 percent are of such poor quality, and they are deemed worthless on arrival and end up dumped in landfill. To simply put, Europe must stop using Africa as dumping-ground for its hazardous waste. African people must give respect and appreciate their local made stuffs rather than preferring western made goods. Attainment of political independence without economic independence is no achievement for Africa.

The continuous loss of human capital due to diseases such as Cholera, Yellow fever, HIV, Ebola Virus Disease (EVD), and the recent Covid-19 incidences and mortality rates should be a wake-up call to Africa continent. Armed conflicts, declining economic policies as a result to government officials looting the public purse, humanitarian crises, huge and colossal foreign debts, human sufferings, deteriorating infrastructure just to mention few, cannot continue to go on. Otherwise, we are not helping to build our own Africa. If we are really looking for a positive change for Africa, then we have to create that Africa we want and must be prepared to sacrifice a great deal of time, energy to build it. Nobody will build Africa for Africans except ourselves. Reaching out for foreign aids in the name of development while diverting such resources into private, and western fat account is rather worsening our own plights. The solution to Africa continent is the dynamic and practical running of African Union with all her resources together in unity, and under one government with one common currency.

Howard Nicholas, an Economist explains how and why the western countries ensure Africa stays poor for the sake of survival of the developed world. According to him, "the Sub-Sahara Africa historically has been fundamental to the prosperity of the advanced countries. As such, Africa has a role to play. Africa has a role as raw material producer. The west will not allow Sub Sahara Africa countries to escape that. The west will do everything to keep Sub Sahara Africa where it is and also impoverished. It is absolutely vital for the prosperity for everyone else so let us get clear about it. This means all economic structures, all global institutions, and economics we teach everyone are all designed to keep Africa exactly where it is and whether it is Europe, or U.S, and or now China, it is always the same. We need Africa to be impoverished because we need those raw materials, and we need them that cheap." What an insult to Africa!!

Howard Nicholas further stated that "It does not mean there is nothing Africa can do. Of course, there is but this is the opposition they are fighting. This is what it is about. Because if Africa does do something different, I assure you the living standards of all those of Europe and Latin America, and Asia is going to fall. And that is a big price to pay. I assure you that the west is not going to allow that without a big fight. Ok, so this is what is fundamentally about."

Dr. Kwame Nkrumah once said that "We must have on our table, what we need today. We must be on the field, working for what we need in 10 years. We must be on the drawing board, planning for what we need in 100 years, and we must be in the classroom, conceptualizing what we need in 1000 years. We have huge deficit, but this generation can rocket to cover every past and present limitations to build a strong bridge for next generations." These ideas of Nkrumah about the future of Africa are still alive even though he is gone. Yet, some of our present leaders of Africa have no clues about the prospects of Africa.

As an African living in the United States, I am offended when some world leaders mocked Africa continent. They are right in whatever they say because of some stupid leaders of Africa. No wonder the west keeps giving financial aids to Africa in order to keep repressing regimes in power. The west will continue lending money to Africa just to indebt Africa. Because the more debts you owe the west, your country will become prisoners and the resources of the countries now belong to them. Somewhere I read that "Poor natural resources governance and management in Africa is a consequence of a complex set of dynamics, which should not be attributed only to foreign multinationals. Our own poor state of governance, rampant corruption and greed in the negotiation of rights to mining, logging or fishing, which are always cloaked in secrecy, is largely responsible." According to Howard Nicholas "We must keep Africa poor at all costs." It means there must be corrupted regimes who are ready to oppress their own citizens. No developmental projects will take place. Just few roads to lead to the raw materials and that is Africa the west want to see. No country can develop without manufacturing, yet some Africa leaders are interested in building mega church buildings for praying after stealing money from state coffers.

An Israeli formal Prime Minister's Derogatory Speech on Africans & Arabs on Nov 14, 2016 "We not obliged even the least to try to prove to anybody and to blacks and Arabs that we are superior people, we have demonstrated that to the black and Arabs in 1001 ways.

The state of Israel we know today is not created by wishful thinking. We have created it at the expenses of intelligence, sweat and blood… We do not pretend like other whites that we like the blacks.

The fact that blacks and Arabs look like human beings do not necessarily make them sensible human beings. Hedgehogs are not porcupines and lizards are not crocodiles because they look alike. If God had wanted us to be equal to black and Arabs, he would have created us all of a uniform color and intellect, but he created us differently whites, blacks, yellow, rulers and the ruled. Intellectually we are superior to the blacks and Arabs that has been proven beyond the reasonable doubt over the years.

I believe that a Jew is honest, God-fearing person who has demonstrated practically the right way of beige. By now everyone of us has seen it practically that blacks and Arabs cannot rule themselves. Give them guns and they will kill each other. They are good in nothing else but making noise, dancing, marrying many wives, alcoholism, witchcraft, indulging in sex, pretending in church, jealousy, fighting and complaining of nonsense.

Let us all accept that the black man is a symbol of poverty, mental inferiority, laziness and emotional incompetence.

Give them money for development they will fight and create hatred and enmity for themselves. This proves to anybody including a stupid fool that Africans don't know what they want. Isn't that plausible?

Therefore, that the white man is created to rule the black man, Africans will always have daydreams. And here is the creature (black man) that lacks foresight but only sees what is near him and still fails to know what to do. A black man is stupid to the extent that he cannot plan for his life beyond a year. Therefore, how can they develop and live longer?

Then which fool argues that the black man is not born a beggar, grows a beggar looks a beggar, falls sick as a beggar and dies a beggar. This has proven beyond reasoning. I wonder that even up to now most Africans still go to school by force and those who are in school are enemies. This is a pregnant stupidity in Africa that needs Jesus's immediate second coming. The body of Africans is very fertile for all diseases in the world because they don't fear even HIV/AIDS. This leaves me with a question, are our eyes created the same with those Africans, I hear there are still cultures in Africa that prohibit them from using latrines which is very annoying.

Please I am sorry to say that I am regretting to say that why did God create Africans. They cried for independence but have failed to rule themselves. For sure being African is a very untreatable disease that even prayers are not enough.

They have minerals but they cannot do anything with it. Therefore, the whites let us go to Africa and pick what we can and leave what is of no use for them. Poverty is a disease to the whites but to the blacks it is very normal. Jesus, please hurry and save Africans and Arabs. A word is enough for the wise." As an African or someone in leadership role, after reading this portion of the book, you need to wake up.

Somewhere I read that "When an African entrepreneur become rich, he will send his money and gold to Switzerland, he is going to France for medical treatment." The alleged quote reads. "He invested in Germany; he is buying houses in Dubai. He consumed Chinese products ..., Praying in Rome or Mecca... Their children are studying in Europe or Canada, and they all take Western Nationalities. They travel to Canada, USA and all over Europe for tourism. If he dies, he will be buried in his home country that he did not care for."

So, when are we going to wake up from our slumber (disunity) and live up to the expectations of our people? We squander all the resources meant for development and rush to church on Sunday to pray to God to conjure automatic funds fall from the supposed heaven to construct roads, modern schools, hospitals, markets, housing etc... Instead of us to build industries, we are building churches and producing fake pastors every year. Our church buildings look like heaven even though I have not been to heaven, and our school building look like refugee camps with all the mineral resources we have. That is why we are insulted as blacks day in day out yet, it looks as if we are still sleeping.

A formal President of the United States referred to African countries, Haiti, and El Salvador as "shithole" nations during a meeting Thursday and asked why the U.S. can't have more immigrants from Norway." Some African leaders all complained that we cannot be referred as "shithole," yet they are corrupt and are not willing to build their individual nations to get out of shitholes.

African energetic youths are often lied to with fake promises of good earnings in the Arab Countries by merciless agents. Passports and other traveling documents are made and when they arrive, they become nothing but domestic slaves, raped, ruthlessly maltreated and are even killed. This is another form of slavery that is going on. It is a well-orchestrated from African countries by the agents all the way to Arab countries. When will Africa Union put a stop to this inhumane form of slavery? If African presidents build factories to create jobs, why should African young girls be domestic workers in the Arab countries? Our young youths need to seek knowledge so that the traffickers cannot deceive them with good paid jobs. The heaven you are being promised in the Arab countries is actually a hell. You will be exhausted by domestic work. Why Africans have to be at the bottom from everywhere? I cannot stand it.

Somewhere I read that" A nation run by bankers will never be out of debt. A nation owned by weapons manufacturers will never know peace. A nation that allows a small segment of its citizens to write the laws will never know justice. And if these elements own the media, we will never know the truth." These are the situations on the ground in some African countries. How can the President of an African country's relatives be appointed as the finance minister and a bunch of other positions in governments? The same minister of finance has his own bank operating. Every money meant for that country is going to end up in his personal bank. This is a conflict of interest and at the same time nepotism. How did this happen? That particular African country is doomed!!!

SOME OBSERVATIONS
IN U.S.A

I have decided to write this book as a result of the positive impact some people have made in my life. I am a son of a cocoa farmer who was raised in the middle of cocoa farm in Akposso Bibi in Togo and is now living in the United States pursuing the American dream. I flew from Ghana to New York and took Greyhound bus from New York to Chicago to meet my sponsor because I did not have enough pocket money to buy a plane ticket to fly from New York to Chicago. To tell you the truth, I did not have enough pocket money on me when I arrived in New York. Because of that, I had to take the bus. While I sat down at home after hard day work, I kept admiring equal job opportunities America has to offer to every qualified person irrespective of where you came from.

I started observing how every system in America works, and it strikes me how my continent is not stepping up to make the union government a priority. Citizens all over the world are rushing to U.S. Embassies to obtain visas for a better life. Democracy is practiced, while human rights, and the rule of law are followed strictly. There is a resilient democratic institution, transparent and peaceful transitions of power after elections. No human being loses his or her life during and after elections are conducted.

It is said that "No country can maintain a rule of law society if its people do not respect the law." The United States is an embodiment of the rule of law in reality. Somewhere I read that "All men are born free and equal, in dignity and in rights, and, being endowed by nature with reason and conscience, they should conduct themselves as brothers one to another." I have seen that testament as I go about doing my job every day. I am aware that "At the institutional level, integrity implies an organization that defines, and acts within, a strong code of ethical conduct and positive values. And adopts no tolerance of attitudes, actions and activities by its employees or partners that deviate from that code." Africa needs therefore, institutional integrity. Presently, we are lacking that ingredient.

While adjusting to American environments after a busy day at work, I quickly observed school shooting, and other mass shootings which occurred quite often. I thought school campuses meant for studies are supposed to be safe. But that have not been the case. Gun uses for recreational hunting is now something else. I understand having a gun at home can ensure your safety against home breakers and also for the sake of security. To see a school child carrying a gun belonging to the parents to school to shoot his or her colleagues is very much alarming.

How can children be allowed to play with a gun in the house? Imagine a high school student coming to school with a loaded gun? I guess some parents even load their guns in the presence of their children. There are so many people who have become victims of gun violence. It is about time the American government tighten firearms acquisitions in order to alleviate gun related incidents just like it is done in

Europe. Some of the causes are attributed to school bullying, teasing, intimidation, anger, rejection, wild video games, broken homes due to divorce, and lack of discipline. Gone are the days where the giant students bully the weaker and feeble ones. Many a times, the weaker ones may be afraid to complain and so they just keep the pain within. Such kids who appeared to be quiet, might be building anger within and the next thing that comes into the mind is revenge and mass shooting.

Watching of scary movies and playing video games can be seen as one of the causes of violent behaviors in school kids. That is just my opinion. Children with drug addicted parents face poor academic functioning, emotional, behavioral, and social problems. Such school kids who are molested, go through physical, and verbal abuses with harsher maltreatment when their parents consume higher rates of alcohol and drugs. Imagine such children who are mentally derailed getting access to gun? The end result may be nothing more than disaster.

Parents should monitor the activities of their kids, closely so as to prevent them from video games that portray aggressive behaviors which can influence their desire to commit murder, torture, shooting. Parental discretion therefore is needed and inevitable. Training, teaching, and disciplining must go hand in hand to the upbringing of our children.

Another observation I made is parents cannot discipline their kids drastically at home. An attempt to discipline your own children the way you want can land you in jail. Kids are taught in school to call 911 on their parents for any least provocation. I think we are over protecting our children by claiming to love them rather. In other part of the world, it takes the whole village to raise a child. An adult neighbor can even discipline you when you are misbehaving in public and later comes to inform your parents. When you dare ask a question to your own kid, he or she can give you a scornful look in the eyes before attempting to give you the answer. You dare take measures to disciple before you know, police will be knocking at your door in the next minute.

At least you should be in position to spank your child for misbehaving. I personally observe my two kids making a mess and walking away from it instead of putting it in the trash bin knowing very well that dad cannot beat them in the old fashion way. I hate kids who eat and live the dishes piling in the sink for whatever time they feel like washing them. It is a fact that some children have been abused terribly by their own parents and stepmothers. I have no remorse for any father or mother who is caught by the law molesting or abusing children. I believe children have to be taught, trained and above all disciplined.

To me, society appears now adays to be worshipping, looking and letting the conscience of the kids dictate rather than the discretion of the parents or guardians. Home is the first line of discipline followed by the school, church, and the society at large. It is imperative for us to continue to teach the accepted ways of and good manners to our children since they constitute our next generation. You want your suffering, toiling and legacy be preserved when you are gone. Society nowadays is over protecting the young ones too much to the extent that the basis of kid's life is fading.

Since too much of everything is bad, parents need to discipline, train, and teach their kids so that when they go out, their behaviors can be checked. We have to control the activities of our children. There must be time to do school assignments, time to watch TV, types of video games to watch, and computer use at home should be monitored. There must be a descent time for kids to go to bed to sleep, well rested for the next day. The most important thing is having both parents being on the same page when it comes to disciplining kids at home.

When parents are not on the same page with regard to disciplining their kids at home, it divides families, foster unhealthy favoritism, and it affects the well-being of the children. Most often, kids see their dad as wicked toward them just because he wants to make sure the right thing is done. Kids see their mother as a savior, loving, lenient and the one who can allow them to do anything without a punishment. You can see clearly how one parent deliberately undermines the other in front of their own kids, resulting to constant disrespect, contempt, and unhealthy future mindset in the kids that it is accepted.

You can imagine how it feels like when you as dad instruct your son to get something done and he has to turn to look at the face of the mother for an eye contact or approval? Should the mother depart the house to work before your kids listen to you or follows your instruction? Or if you cannot tell your kids of what to do while their mother is the house, then we have a problem. These are the seeds of disrespect one parent is sowing into the family. Husband and wife can sometimes argue in front of their kids and respect each other. But when your wife can boldly slap you in front of the kids in the course of arguing, you can image the level of disrespect, and division she is sowing in the kids about their father.

When one parent can allow their kids to get away with behaviors, and attitudes that the other parent would discipline them for, that is very bad and unhealthy. Children uses one parent against the other with loopholes just from their observations between mom and dad. For example, when your children know that there are one set of rules when their dad is away (mother's rule) and another set of rules when their father comes back home from work, that is a recipe for a disaster.

Peer influence may be a factor to your child's good or bad behavior. As it is often said "show me your friend and I will tell you your character." Parents are requested to take all precautions in making sure something good comes out of their kids. Bad influence usually may lead to your child's doom. Your teen girl provocative manners of dressing must be checked since it can attract attention from wrong boys and some older men.

It can be an indicative of having inappropriate relationship with guys by showing her skin as being beautiful. Your teenage girl will crash with you over too tight shirt, skirt too short, and a dress that is too revealing. Don't make them feel shameful but find a way to talk to them about their choices and the consequences of their actions. Children still need to learn about character training, self-control, obedience, and self-discipline. These good values are still phasing out in the so-called modern kids. The above discussions are some of my observations in the U.S and my point of view about how things ought to be.

Since I came to U.S and joined the Navy, I have been bombarded with several questions about Africa and I found it difficult to understand. I don't know whether such people are merely ignorant or are naïve about Africa continent. A cross section of people living in America want to know if we have cities in Africa. Some people wanted to know how Africans cope up with life on a daily basis with all wild animals walking on the street. Do Africans sleep in a house or in trees? Do you guys have roads and hotels? How do you manage to speak English Language perfectly with your accent? A friend from Nigeria whom I met in A school in Texas at the Air force Base was asked by one female whether he came to U.S before starting to wear shoes. A white woman I know expressed her interests to travel to Africa just to go and see animals. She even asked me to know why I came to America while there are beautiful animals in Africa.

When people asked me such provoking questions about Africa, they would then say, don't get me wrong, it is because he or she watched a documentary on Discovery Channel or National Geographic Channel. I don't know where to start from, but it sounds mind troubling to know that Some Americans, and even kids think that Africa continent is all about wild animals, forests and vast lands. Africa is not about monkeys, giraffes, lions, elephants. Africa is about 54 countries which suffered from slavery, to colonialism, and all the way to independence. Africa continent used to be under the umbrella of Organization of Africa Unity (OAU), but now known as Africa Union (AU).

African people don't sleep with animals, nor do they sleep in the bush, on trees with monkeys, and lions. You have to go to the zoo in order to see animals in any civilized country. Each country has a capital, other cities and maybe it is a political propaganda on the part of the western media to degrade and humiliate the people of Africa. It is just like how African Americans and the diaspora blacks are suffering from discrimination in the United States. A ten-year-old girl whom I have been introduced to for the first time as an African, wants to go to Africa to see lions, tigers, and monkeys. It was shocking and surprising to me but it has been the same mind game to dehumanize what is good about Africa.

A Sailor on one of the ships I have been stationed asked me how does it feel to come from the jungle and now in U.S Navy? He was referring smartly to coming from Africa as the jungle just because that is what the western media have shown centuries about Africa. You can imagine the same Africa the western nations came to do slave trade, divided them among themselves, colonized and now turning around to call it the jungle.

You would be amazed to know that a lot of people living in America don't know that Africa is a continent. Some too don't know how many countries we have in Africa continent, let alone know that life goes on normally in Africa. Just like people wake up in America and go to work and to return to their homes to shower, eat, watch television, and then go to bed. It is about time the western media show both the nice and bad places. It needs to be clear that while the United States is in union government, Africa Union has fifty-four countries. However, Africa Union countries have not yet opened their borders practically to each other, Their currencies also differ unlike America has a strong dollar. As a result of this, each country is an individual nation with her own sovereignty. I don't know when the union government will open borders across the continent to enable free flow of trade and movement of their own people for a better life.

I can just pick up my car key and go for a ride from one state to another freely without any police barrier in the United States. But that is not possible in Africa yet. They have a lot of barriers and check points you have to pass through. Movement of goods and human beings across borders are subject to tough custom and immigration rules. These are countries divided by the western colonial masters like France, Britain, Portugal, etc. Some countries speak the English language while others speak French, and Swahili as colonial official languages. I hope to be alive to see Africa using one passport, one currency, and borders opened for continental free trade. Dr. Kwame Nkrumah once said that "The people of Africa are crying for unity." Nkrumah also dreamed of United States of Africa with harmonized systems, dismantled boundaries and more intra-African trade before he was removed from power in 1966.

Another observation was having an accent as an immigrant in America seems to be a mockery to some

Americans. Some people don't know that when you speak more than one language, you turn to have a dynamic and a rich cultural heritage. Since immigrants speak different languages, they have a strong accent whenever they are speaking. You would be amazed to know that some people living in America think that because you have accent, it means you don't know how to speak good English.

Some of my Sailors on the ship told me that they are shocked when I speak good English even though I come from Africa. I pondered over and deduced that they were not expecting me to express myself very well in English. What a world are we living in and what are we teaching our generation about other parts of the world apart from America? Or what kind of subjects do they learn in school? It is about time the western media stopped portraying Africa continent as the land of animals.

Life goes on normally in Africa like any other place of the world. It means people wake up and go to work, and kids go to school. There are roads, airports, beaches, and hospitals. If you want to see wild animals, you have to go to the zoos to see them. Lions, giraffes, and monkeys are not walking on the streets of Africa like how it is deeply rooted in the mind of some people in America. As a developing continent, Africa countries are still building schools, roads, bridges, modern markets, hospitals, housings etc. They are also extending electricity to the remote areas of their countries and providing portable water to their communities. You must understand that developed nations have already finished doing all these amenities and other infrastructures. These are some of the differences we have between the biggest, and richest continent (Africa) and the developed ones. As an African born and raised in Togo before continuing my education in Ghana, I have never seen lions or any wild animals walking on the street of Africa. Yet I have to get such questions throughout my Navy career on the ship and on shore duties. It is very disturbing, and I entreat the youth, the older ones too to use the internet to be abreast with Africa continent.

An African America female I worked with in the Navy wanted to know whether there is no fork, spoon, or knife in Africa? According to her, she has seen Africans using their hands to eat food and she found it disgusting and unhygienic. Another person said that he thought Africa is just a vast land of forest. My question to her was why there are thousands of spoons, forks, and knives in the U.S, yet Americans use their fingers to eat burgers? She could not answer my question but to say that I was mean to her.

I observed that a cross-section of people are ignorant about Africa and are ready to look down upon you once they hear that you are from Africa. The African people are not stupid as perceived by some westerners based on what the media shows about Africa. As far as I know, every society has its own culture. As such, things are not done the same way in two different societies. The last time I checked the definition of culture, it said "A culture is a way of life of a group of people—the behaviors, beliefs, values, and symbols that they accept, generally without thinking about them, and are passed along by communication and imitation from one generation to the next." The culture of one society may include the way the people talk, eat, dance, and other accepted ideas.

The notion that the people of Africa are primitive in some western communities is a serious mistake. A mere look at your face or when you begin to talk with an accent, it sends a signal to some people born in the United States automatically that such a person is a complete novice, naïve or ignorant from Africa. I am an African born and raised in Ghana and Togo before coming to the States in 2000. Despite all the problems Africa is facing right now with their corrupt leaders, the youth are awakening, and living as citizens and not spectators. I edge the youth to continue to register their displeasure against their government neglect of their area development, deplorable roads, schools, hospitals, housing, lack of toilet facilities, potable water, overflowing refuge dump etc...

We are developing, even though we are far behind, we shall get there. We have to continue to create more awareness, more educations, and exposes our corrupts government officials to do the needful developments with state money. We need to hold government officials otherwise known as political thieves responsible, and demand uttermost accountability, and transparency.

The fact that my brothers, sisters, and I grew up in a village in Togo before we went to Ghana to continue, we have never seen a lion even in the village. But one thing I certainly know is that all wild animals are kept in the zoo. Just like in in the United States, you have to visit the zoo in order to see animals, the same way it is done in Africa too. Your media go to the game reserve and national park to make documentaries. Tell them to show you the cities of Africa nations. I hope you learned something meaningful about Africa you perceived in your mind as compared to the real nations you don't see on your television in America.

HUMILITY

According to Merrian-Webster, humility is "freedom from pride or arrogance; the quality or state of being humble." Humility is often characterized as genuine gratitude and a lack of arrogance, a modest view of oneself. There are those who believe that the Bible has something good for them all the time. As such, they humble from the beginning all the way to the end of their blessings. There are others who also think that the Bible has something good for them at the time they are in need. So, they humble themselves to get what they need and once they get what they need from you, then they would change their attitudes toward you.

Such people call on Almighty God and go to church frequently and pray several times for their prayers to be answered. When the good Lord finally grants them their heart desires, they think that is the last time they have to call on God. Such people begin to make silly mistakes. The good Lord is not stupid. The same God that answers your prayers is still going to watch you. He wants to see if you have wisdom and whether you are trustworthy and thankful.

When our father in Heaven grants your heart desire, it is just the first stage of your happiness. It is like getting a help from other people while climbing the tree in order to get to the top. Getting to the top of the tree does not mean you should forget about the help you received on your way to get there. Those who failed to recognize the very people who helped them at a point in time will definitely pay a heavy price by nature for doing so.

Don't be like some church goers who are not actual Christians. Some people just get dressed gorgeously to show off at church on Sundays. They pray loudly, dance as if they are true and actual Christians. When their name is mentioned, everyone says good things about them. He or she is a good boy or good girl. He or she is a god fearing with good moral character that is all you will be hearing from onlookers. They hold themselves in high esteem, thereby establishing public trust in the community where they reside at. If you know what they are planning to do as soon as the good Lord lifts them up high, you will be amazed.

When circumstances prompt you to travel out of your country of origin to an unknown place in a quest for a better life, you will meet, or hear the stories of the so-called Christians who were the angels in their formal countries. Such moments have series of stories to tell in one way or the other. In case you are planning to travel for a greener pasture somewhere apart from your land of birth, you have to be prepared to face the challenges. The place you intend to go may seem all greener but wait until you get there and find out for yourself. The previous people who have been there may not tell you much about their experiences. Some people will polish it to look like you don't have to work in order to earn a living. Whenever you hear such stories, you need to think again, perhaps, they are deceiving you.

Here you are at the long last in foreign land with the help of relatives, loved ones, uncles, father, husbands, and wife. Don't begin to carry out selfish and secret plans than the ones that brought you to the foreign land. There are situations where loved ones petition their relatives to join them and as soon as they arrive through the airport, they depart to their own secret planned destinations. Others will arrive with your help and wait until you equally help them to receive their working documents and then, they will start announcing to you their true characters. These are the very people who are angels, and fake or true Christians in their original country.

Never forget about three types of people in your life. People who helped you in your difficult time, people who left you in your difficult times and people who put you in difficult time. Also, never trust a person that has let you down more than two times. Once was a warning, twice was a lesson and anything more than that is simply taking advantage of you. When you come to a point where you have no need to impress anybody, your freedom will begin. Beware of your friends and people in general. The good you do today to someone may be forgotten tomorrow. Some of them are really friends to count on while others are faked. Once they stop talking to you, then they start talking about you. Sometimes, you just have to learn to keep your mouth shut in order to survive and never look down on anyone in life.

The era of God-fearing person has become something of the past. Some claim to be respectful, faithful, beautiful, handsome and the idea is just to play you. Wait until they are settled and comfortable where they want to be with your help and see. You will be sorry of that Christian boy or girl in the next door. It is no longer worthy to give someone who pretends to love your precious time, attention let alone love. Some of them pretend to smile at you yet they don't care about you. They are only there to use you in order to get to where they need to be.

Sometimes, the actual people who are meant for each other don't complain about time being too long. Don't let people or circumstances upset you. Try to rise above every difficulty, knowing that Almighty God has given you the power to remain calm even though it is not easy to do so. I know it is difficult thing to ask but try to live your life in happiness, bloom where you are planted, and allow Jehovah God to fight your battles for you.

Never give up easily!!! Never lose hope either. Always have faith of that which is coming but is not yet here, for it will allow you to cope up. Trying times are real but will pass as they always do. Just have patience which I will refer to as the most important ingredient. Your dreams will come true. Put on a smile and you will live or endure through your pain or agony. Know that all things will pass, and you will regain your strengths. Just don't forget about where you come from. The downfall of some people is because they have forgotten of where they came from just after the Lord has lifted them. There is no victory without a pain.

It is a wise saying that: "don't ever feel bad for making a decision about your own life that upsets other people." You are not responsible for their happiness. You are responsible for your own happiness. Anyone who wants you to live in misery for their happiness should not be in your life to begin with. When people throw you stones, it is because you are a good tree full of fruits. They see a lot of harvest in you. Don't go down to their level by throwing them back stones but throw them your fruits so that the seeds of yourself may inspire them to change their ways.

When God blesses you financially, don't just raise your standard of living and forget about where you came from to get to where you are now. There are always those who do go down such paths and regret later. Don't be one of them.

Never push a loyal person to the point where they no longer care. Someday in the future, everything will make a perfect sense. So, for now, laugh at the confusion, smile through the tears and keep reminding yourself that everything happens for a reason. When you come to a point where you have no need to impress anybody then your freedom will begin. Happiness will keep you sweet while trial will keep you strong. Sorrows will keep you human and failures will keep you humble. And Almighty God will keep you going through all battles.

When you want to help, do it because it's in your heart. Not because you want something in return. There is a school of thought that coming together is just the beginning. While keeping together, it is unity we stand and for that matter progress and as such we must work together to fix human problems. Life is too short to worry about what others say or think about you. You need to have fun and give them something to talk about. With the experience some of us have gone through, never give up and never lose hope. Always have faith which will allow you to cope up. Trying times will definitely pass as they always do. The most important thing to share with you is to have patience as your dreams are about to come true. It is said that "put on a smile, because you will live through your pain."

An opportunity came my way and I grabbed it firmly to travel to the United States of America for a greener pasture. My observations are what I am writing. Anybody who want to travel under the sponsorship of someone to the Western countries need to get fully prepared before embarking on such journeys. Some people are anxious to travel, in the process, come to mess up with their precious life in a far place. Going back home with an empty hand is not an option. The going gets tough and they end up indulging in dubious things which they would not have ventured if they were to stay in their country of origin.

To be able to immigrate to America with one pair of shoes and one traveling bag and settled and in turn sponsor someone to join you is often seen as good idea. The person you are sponsoring to join you on the other hand, is already planning how he or she will trick you when he or she finally arrives. They often pretend to be good persons or strong Christians in order to get all the financial help. Once they join you and receive all the necessary working documents through you the sponsor, then they start to change gradually.

Eventually, they will not listen to you again. Some relatives and loved ones will wait to get a job then you will start noticing some unusual behaviors and tactics in them. Some of them will intentionally make a mess so that you can complain about it. Once you complain, then they start pouring the insults on you. And in the process, they will now let you know how they don't like you but have used you to get to the end of their destinations. The number of years they have to wait for the immigration documents and your financial supports during those years have become things of the past.

Somewhere I read that "It is bad enough when a stranger or foe betrays you, but when it is someone, you believed, to be a close and trusted friend, partner, or spouse, it is especially hurtful. It might feel like you were taken advantage of, deceived, humiliated, despised, cheated, or stabbed in the back." So, the closer you are to another person, the more opportunity there is likely for friction to occur between the two of you.

There are people in life who just pretend to like, love and respect you just because they want to get something from you or use you to arrive at their destinations. Such people are lively, smiling and humble before the society in which they live in. They are considered the holy, sacred and above all respectful. The betrayal is where the offender breaks the trust or expectations of the bond in some ways. You will meet such people whether you like it or not.

The very people you are helping have their own ambition set up long time and are just waiting for a perfect opportunity. Others are greedy and calling you stupid and naïve. You are not my type, and you don't qualify to tell me what to do. He or she just wants to pass through you for a better life. Some close relatives of yours just want what you have, while others see you as an impediment in their way of what is needed. Imagine when you a teacher, and you are not qualified to date a certain girl. But once you the same teacher wins a visa lottery to travel, now you are qualified to date that same girl who rejected you earlier. Those who pretend to love you are just looking out for their own interests.

The person you spent your money on for years to join you can now cook and eat and tell you if you are hungry, you should go the kitchen to find something to eat. When you asked that relative what did you cook after coming from work, you are in trouble. You can get a response like; did you bring me here to be your maid servant? All of sudden, that person attitudes begin to change toward you because he or she now possesses the Green Card, Social Security Number, and Work Authorization through you as the host. The message to you is that he or she has gotten what they want, and you are no longer needed. They don't love or care about you but just to pretend to get everything they need from you. Be aware of them and don't be fooled twice. The same people you helped at a point in time are going to be the very ones to betray you.

As an immigrant who came to United States on 4th July 2000, I heard of American Dream. I asked of the meaning, and it was explained to me as "the belief that anyone, regardless of where they were born or what class they were born into, can attain their own version of success." Others referred to it as "A happy way of living that is thought of by many Americans as something that can be achieved by anyone in the U.S. especially by working hard and becoming successful." There is, therefore, this idea that hard work will pay off and can lead to increased stability and class position in America.

So American dream mostly feel like promises kept if only you are ready to work hard and consistently. As immigrant with few dollars in my pocket, poverty, pain, and frustration, I was optimistic of better, and a brighter future having been told of American dream. For some youths in America who claimed that life is hard here, my message for you is that you just have to work hard. I must say that this type of American dream cannot happen in Africa continent where I come from.

There is a high spirit of optimism, joy, and the decency from hard work irrespective of your color, religion, and where you come from. I wish American dream is available in my country of origin—Ghana. You can get a job without even having a college degree. Guess what -you can even get a loan to buy a house, and a car. You cannot even tell the difference between the rich and the poor person in America. America dreams therefore will give you a better life and I worked hard in the Navy, and I am proud Veteran now enjoying from my portion of American dreams.

At this point, I want to thank you dear reader of this book. You may not agree with me in everything that I have written in this book. Everybody is entitled to his or her opinions. If you meet someone on your way in life that needs help, don't hesitate to do so. While you help that person, don't expect an immediate reward. Allow Almighty God to reward your efforts at the right time. Humble yourself and the Lord of nature will lift you high. Be respectful and don't become arrogant because you have gotten to the top. Don't forget that no condition is permanent. I wish you dear reader of this book all the best in life.

www.ingramcontent.com/pod-product-compliance
Lightning Source LLC
Chambersburg PA
CBHW020444130626
46549CB00001B/287